the SECRET LANGUAGE of Horses

Books of Merit

2012.

Happy Christmas Andrea
I love the pictures, hope
you do too.
Woobie, BoBo & I are just
delighted to have you back.
much love, Maaa.

the SECRET LANGUAGE of Horses

THE BODY LANGUAGE OF EQUINE BODIES

Heather Dunphy

THOMAS ALLEN PUBLISHERS
TORONTO

Library and Archives Canada Cataloguing in Publication

Dunphy, Heather, 1972-
The secret language of horses : the body language of equine bodies / Heather Dunphy.

Includes bibliographical references and index.
ISBN 978-0-88762-935-8

1. Horses. 2. Horses--Behavior. 3. Human-animal communication. I. Title.

SF285.3.D85 2012 636.1'083 C2011-907119-3

Published by Thomas Allen Publishers,
a division of Thomas Allen & Son Limited,
390 Steelcase Road East
Markham, Ontario, L3R 1G2 CANADA

www.thomasallen.ca

Conceived, designed, and produced by:
Quid Publishing
Level 4 Sheridan House
114 Western Road
Hove BN3 1DD
England
www.quidpublishing.com

Design: Ali Walper
Cover image: © Janahorova | Dreamstime

10 9 8 7 6 5 4 3 2 1

Printed and bound in Singapore

CONTENTS

HORSES THROUGHOUT HISTORY

THE HORSE AND HUMAN BOND

The relationship between domestic horses and humans began approximately 6,000 years ago, with equine hoofprints leading the way to advancements in agriculture, warfare, communication, transportation, travel, and trade. Horsepower contributed to food cultivation, making it possible for people to evolve from nomadic food gatherers to settled farmers. It also transformed the battlefield, helping to destroy some empires while building others. It made communication and travel between distant lands possible, which facilitated the sharing of ideas. No other domestic animal has had such an impact on the development of civilization.

All good things take time and this holds true for the equine, with the modern horse 55 to 60 million years in the making. Experts may not all be in agreement as to when the earliest ancestor of today's horse first came on the scene, but they agree that these horses did not resemble today's equine. Instead they were small dog-sized animals, gradually evolving into the horses we have today. Originating in North America, horses spread to other parts of the world, until they were made almost extinct during the Ice Age. During this time they disappeared from the Americas but continued to evolve in Eurasia. They did not return to America until the Age of Discovery when, in 1494, horses were brought over on a Spanish ship—some say by explorer Christopher Columbus, on his second voyage to the New World.

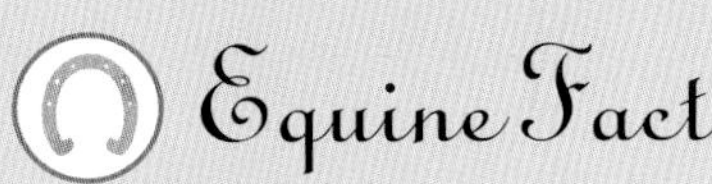

At one time, horses of many colors, shapes, and sizes roamed the world, most of them the size of a large dog.

The relationship between humans and equines did not get off to a good start, from the equine's point of view. Prehistoric people were predators of the horse, seeing them only as a food source. With domestication the relationship changed, but domestication of the horse did not come easily. Despite their willingness to follow a leader, the speed and stamina of the horse meant that, for the most part, they were able to remain out of human reach. Domestication only occurred about 6,000 years ago—substantially later than other farm animals—and since then humans and horses have been powerfully linked. Horses revolutionized the cultures that adopted them and shaped history, bringing about significant advancements in agriculture, travel, trade, warfare, and communication.

Today, equines no longer fight our battles or plow our fields, but, with more than 58 million horses in the world today, the strong bond between horse and human continues.

BEHIND THE SIGNS

Lost in Translation?

If you are positioned near your horse's flank then your horse's ear may be facing back. Ears pointing back as opposed to pinned or flattened stiffly back can be "saying" two very different things. The distinctions may be subtle, but observation will teach you to recognize pinned ears (fear or aggression) versus pointed ears (contentment or attention). It's important to look at the big picture when translating your horse's body language, and to learn what the nuances of his behavior may mean.

FARMING

Horses were initially valued for their meat and milk, and then for their ability to carry the loads of the nomadic farmer. As more farmers settled, and the cultivation of grain became common, the role of the horse expanded. Not merely a food source, the horse became a means of increasing food production by working the land. Pulling plows, herding animals, powering the grindstones that made flour from grain—these advancements in agriculture were all based on horsepower. Some experts posit that this marked a change in human development, from food gatherers to food producers.

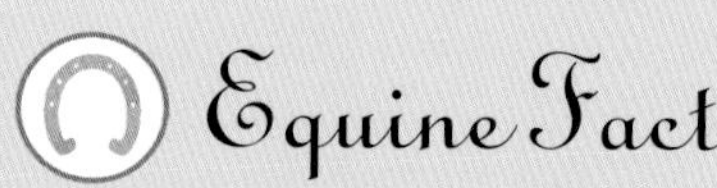

Horse milk continues to be enjoyed by people in parts of the world, including Kazakhstan and Mongolia, where it is fermented into alcohol.

WARFARE

The significance of the horse in exploration and the building and maintaining of empires cannot be overstated. Nations rose and fell thanks to the horse. The history of warfare shows that those with mounted cavalries had an advantage on the battlefield, which translated to greater opportunity to stockpile, plunder, and increase influence. Horses are fast and maneuverable, and capable of covering extensive ground. Soldiers on horseback and horse-driven chariots made intimidating opponents. The armies of Genghis Khan and Alexander the Great both used horses in the military to great effect.

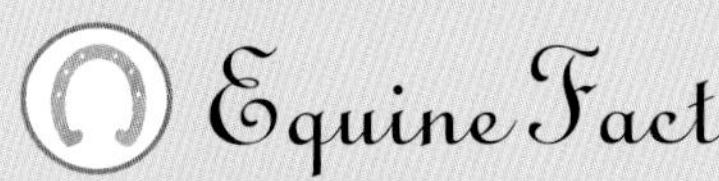

Today, police forces continue to employ horses for crowd and riot control because of their maneuverability, and their ability to both calm and intimidate.

However, a cavalry was expensive, as the Romans could confirm. With their empire already financially overburdened, they were forced to switch from infantry to cavalry in order to stand a fighting chance against the enemies they kept losing against. Unfortunately, the enormous expense contributed to the fall of their empire.

COMMUNICATION

As the only mode of swift travel and communication available at the time, horses also helped to maintain empires in periods of peace. They enabled rulers to communicate with all corners of their lands, and to keep control of their far-flung territories. One example of this is the Persian empire; because of its vast size, many believe that it could not have existed were it not for the advances in travel and communication made possible by the horse. Until the introduction of steam engines and the telegraph, there was simply no other viable option.

BEHIND THE SIGNS

Courier Legacy

"Neither snow nor rain nor heat nor gloom of night stays these couriers from the swift completion of their appointed rounds"; so goes a passage from *The Histories* by Herodotus, written from the 450s to the 420s BCE. It describes the mounted couriers of the Persian Empire, who would not have been able to maintain swift communication across the empire without horses. It is often cited inaccurately as the motto of the US postal service. It is, however, inscribed all around the outside of the New York City General Post Office, a historic landmark occupying two city blocks.

TRAVEL

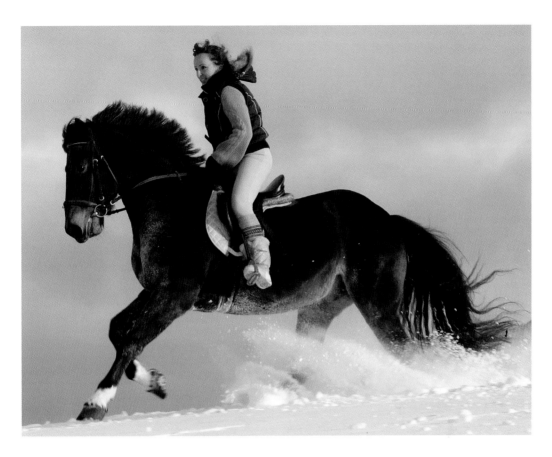

The domestication of the horse meant that long distances, previously unthinkable for a journey, became manageable. Humans, whose range had been limited, now had a better, far-reaching mode of transport. This enabled migration to lands of better opportunity—for example, to escape drought—for those who could afford horse-travel.

Travel is said to broaden the mind, and so it is interesting to note that the domestication of the horse loosely coincided with the end of the Dark Ages. Horse-travel meant it was possible to encounter other cultures, which in turn provided opportunities to exchange ideas with people of different backgrounds and experiences. It also made trade possible between these extended communities, facilitating the transport of previously unheard-of merchandise and technologies. This resulted in a greater body of collective knowledge, and increased sophistication in early societies. Stagecoaches, mail coaches, and wagons revolutionized travel—all of which were powered by the horse.

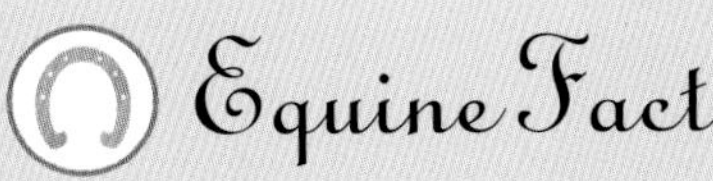

Equine Fact

Early civilizations reared horses to fight battles and plow fields. In return, horses shaped history.

LEISURE

Horses did more than work farms and win battles. They were also reared for pleasure in ancient times, just as they are today. Hunting, for sport or table, and racing were popular leisure activities, with the Persians and Greeks thought to be the first to institute horse racing, followed by the Romans. In the Middle Ages, mounted tournaments became popular. They provided entertainment and kept knights in fighting form, ready for the next battle.

BEHIND THE SIGNS

Domestication Timeline

Although most historians and zoologists agree that domestication of the horse began approximately 6,000 years ago, some claim it began when humans first started breeding horses. Others look to when the horse was first harnessed or mounted. Archaeological evidence has helped to draw up an approximate timeline of the horse, which shows that numerous breeds were domesticated and employed for manual labor.

No. 1

HORSE-TO-HORSE

HERD DYNAMICS

An understanding of the why and how of the herd—its function, social structure, and language—is necessary in order to understand our equines. Whether wild or domesticated, the herd instinct is deeply rooted, and the dynamics of the herd help to explain horse behavior.

The "why" of the herd can be answered in one word: survival. This can be further broken down into safety, the search for food and water, and reproduction—all things that the herd facilitates. As prey animals, there is safety in numbers. Multiple sets of eyes looking out for predators are better than one set of eyes. At more vulnerable times—such as night, when their vision is compromised—horses will gather together, watchful as they graze. The daylight hours, when the horse's visual field is stronger, offers an opportunity for the majority of the herd to take time out to rest, leaving the remaining horses on sentry duty. And in case of a predator attack, being one of many lessens the odds of being the one caught.

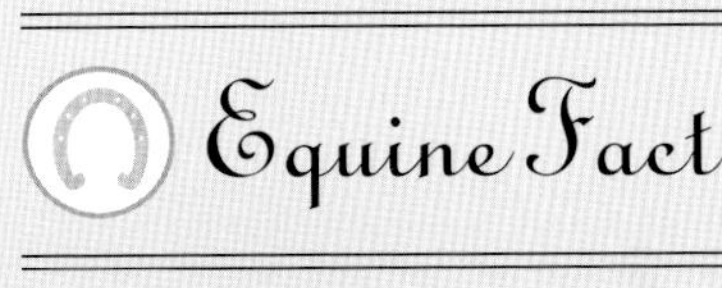

Today the horse's only natural predator is the mountain lion, also known as the puma or cougar.

The herd, or band of horses, is most often a small group. It's made up of the dominant stallion—the alpha—who is usually six years or older, with up to six mares and their offspring. This harem-like herd structure ensures a stable reproductive unit by providing the stallion with mares close at hand, so there is no need to travel to seek out a mate. The alpha is responsible for the safety of the herd, and when roaming will most often be found at the rear, keeping the slower horses moving with the rest of the group. There will typically be a dominant mare who establishes areas for feeding and leads the group in grazing.

A hierarchy keeps the herd functioning, with the dominant stallion at the top of the pecking order. The next in rank is often determined by a variety of factors such as age, length of time with the herd, and aggressiveness. The bond between herd members is strong, with individual friendships within the group. They will groom each other, nibbling at each other's necks and backs, with those higher in rank protecting their friends at the bottom of the hierarchy. The herd acts as an extended family, with the young cared for by all.

It's helpful to remember that, while horses do not generally care where they stand in the pecking order, it is important that they are aware of it nonetheless. Fights for dominance occur only when the leader does not have the respect and trust of the other horse, which causes uneasiness amongst the herd. When ranking is clear, horses are content. Once roles are established, violence within the group is unusual, although body language may be used to signify displeasure or warning (see chapter 6). However, if the rules of the herd are broken, the offending horse may be driven off or moved from the center of the herd—the safest area—to the fringes, where they are more vulnerable to predator attack and the elements.

NEIGHBORING HERDS

Herds are nonterritorial and will often live near other bands of horses. Although they may share the same territory, two herds will maintain a respectful distance. The dominant stallion of each herd sends clear messages to the other herds that his mares are off limits. They do this by "rounding up" their mares to show dominance. Or, they urinate on the droppings of mares from their own herd, to send a message of ownership and warning to other stallions.

FORMING A HERD

The alpha is the only one who sires the herd's offspring, so when young males reach full sexual maturity they are ousted. This is typically before the age of three, at which time these colts form a bachelor group of up to three male horses. They exist on the fringes of herds, until each is able to form its own. This is made possible in three ways: young females, fillies, leave their foundation herd because they are sent away; fillies choose to leave once they come into estrous (their heat cycle) and are able to reproduce, usually at around age two; or the young stallion is able to gain dominance over the older stallion of another herd.

BEHIND THE SIGNS

Time to Go

Experts believe that inbreeding is avoided in wild horses because they encourage their young to leave the herd upon reaching sexual maturity. Colts are sent away before the age of three, to prevent them from breeding within the herd they were born into. Fillies may also leave once they are able to reproduce. New herds are eventually formed, made up of equines from different foundation herds. As a result, these horses are more genetically diverse than domestic horses and are better able to adapt and survive in the wild.

BEHIND THE SIGNS

"I'm in Charge Now"

As part of the herd, the human leader must earn alpha status just as a wild horse would: through consistency, clear communication, and care. To build a bond, your horse needs to trust you. If he is confused by your mixed messages, frustration, or volatility, he will not see you as the leader. Alphas don't need to scream. If your horse doesn't respect you, he won't follow you. He'll see himself as the leader—after all, someone has to do it! This is a problem that many new owners experience, but it is one that can be fixed. Let your horse know by tone and action that you are in charge, and he will come to believe it. In return he'll give you his trust, one of the most gratifying gifts a horse owner could receive.

HERD INSTINCT IN DOMESTIC HORSES

The domesticated herd is often separated into groups when in pasture to prevent problematic dominance issues—mares in one field, with geldings (castrated males) in another. Both are kept apart from the stallion to prevent unwanted breeding with mares and unwanted fighting between the males. Social ranking still occurs, but the human in charge should be the alpha.

Today's domestic horse does not need the herd in the same way their wild ancestors did, yet they are nevertheless hardwired to live as part of a group. Their safety is provided for, yet companionship is just as important a need. Other horses are the best bet for providing this, as interaction with members of their own species makes for happier and better-adjusted equines. If this is not possible then the presence of other hoofed animals (such as goats, sheep, or donkeys) are necessary for their well-being. Plenty of human companionship is a given. It is a basic care requirement and responsibility of horse ownership.

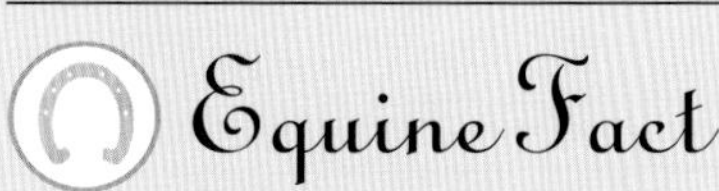

The hierarchy of the herd has greatly benefitted humans. Without it we would not have the relationship with equines we have today, as the horse's willingness to follow an alpha is what made domestication possible.

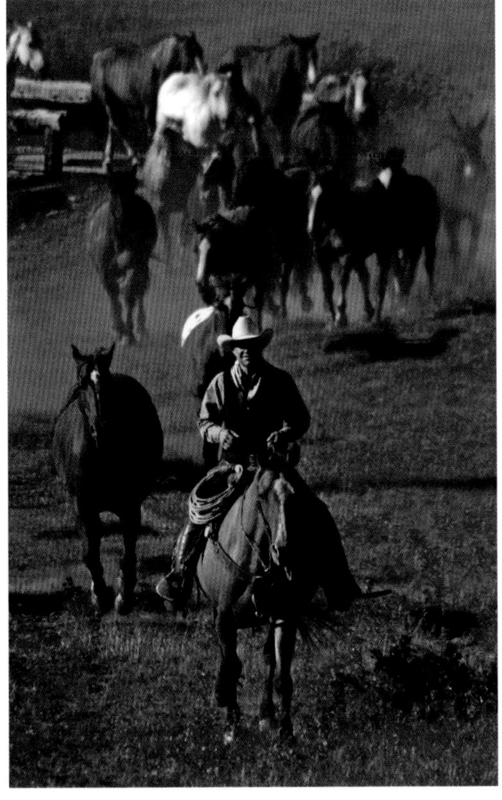

Equine Fact

Herd instinct is inherited, and is an integral part of equine behavior.

The alpha is not the leader because he is the strongest, meanest member of the herd, nor is the submissive herd member necessarily the physically weakest. True alpha leadership is about attitude, and is gained through trust. This is achieved by consistently and clearly communicating with your horse. Empathy is a must—an understanding that your horse has different needs and communication methods. He may speak a foreign language, but it's a language we can learn. And the return on investment is great, as any horse lover will attest.

Equines are social creatures and are not meant to live alone. Their modern herd consists of the people and animals in their life. If deprived of this they, will often develop behavioral disorders (see chapter 18).

Leader or follower? Wild horses need to know their place in the herd hierarchy, and this is true for the domestic horse too. As a member of the herd, the owner or handler must establish leadership, otherwise the horse may step into the alpha role. That makes their human lower in rank—not conducive to training or a good relationship!

No. 2

HORSE SENSE

EQUINES' INTERACTION WITH THEIR ENVIRONMENT

Like people, horses see, smell, hear, touch, and taste. Unlike people, horses are not hunters but prey, and so the way in which their senses developed differs from ours. Domestication has also played its part, dulling some senses that once helped wild horses flee from predators and danger. An understanding of the differences between how horses and people interpret the world translates to a better understanding of why horses act as they do, and how to communicate more effectively with them.

EYES AND VISION

Horses rely heavily on their vision. The narrowness of their head combined with the distance between their eyes results in an almost 180-degree field of vision in each eye. This allows equines to see an incredibly wide area—almost a panoramic view—around them. Despite this impressive field of vision, horses have a blind spot directly behind them, which is why they should never be approached in this way. It can frighten them and, as prey animals, they may instinctively react with flight, which can be a danger to them and to you.

Although the horse has monocular vision (meaning his two eyes work independently, each covering a wide area and seeing different objects) and binocular vision, allowing him to focus on an object with both eyes, the latter comes with a processing delay of seconds in which the horse identifies what he sees. This explains why horses may startle at objects that seem innocuous to us. With eyes that are generally 8–10 inches (20–25 cm) apart, a horse may see something clearly with his left eye that he doesn't see with his right eye until he approaches it. Unable to identify what he's suddenly seeing with both eyes for the few seconds in which the image is processed, he may shy away from it—the reaction of a prey animal to something that surprises or frightens him.

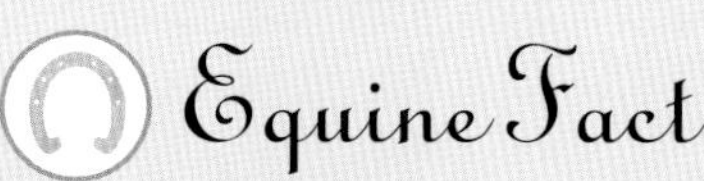

Equine Fact

Sudden, unfamiliar, and fast movement can "spook" a horse. Equines that shy, or startle, frequently may benefit from being given a few extra seconds to use their binocular vision, allowing them more time to understand what's expected of them.

SMELL AND TASTE

Scent allows horses to communicate with other equines, sniff out trouble, and distinguish what is safe to eat. They greet each other with their noses, filing away the scent for future reference so they can identify other horses in a crowd. A whiff of danger from the scent of a predator will get a horse moving in a hurry, just as the smell of certain foliage will cause the horse to avoid or enjoy it.

Scent is so integral to horses that they have organs at the top of their mouth, known as Jacobson or vomeronasal organs. The flehmen response—when the horse curls back his lips and seems to grimace with his mouth open—sends pheromones and other scents to the Jacobson organ, through which equines are able to analyze scent molecules inhaled through their mouth, rather than relying on nose alone. This flehmen response is typically seen when a new smell is experienced for the first time.

To communicate that you are a friend not a foe, extend the back of your hand when you approach a horse, letting them sniff at you.

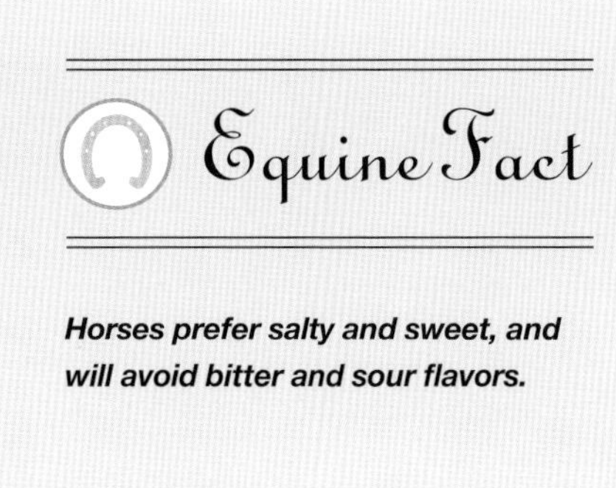

Equine Fact

Horses prefer salty and sweet, and will avoid bitter and sour flavors.

BEHIND THE SIGNS

Communication Through the Senses

Let your horse know you're there by letting him see you. If you must move behind him and into his blind spot, keep a hand on him and speak to him, to remind him through touch and sound of your presence. Avoid heavy perfumes, so that your horse gets to know your scent. Give your horse a rubdown or massage. All of this sends a message to your horse, strengthening your bond and improving your communication.

TOUCH

Have you ever watched a horse's tail swish at a fly that has suddenly landed on his body? This is no accident. It results from the nerve endings that cover the horse's epidermis, which make their skin sensitive to even the lightest touch.

Riders "talk" to their horse through touch, communicating where and when to go. Miscommunication arises when the rider is not consistent in their touch or weight shift, resulting in a frustrated and confused horse—one who ignores instructions or misinterprets them.

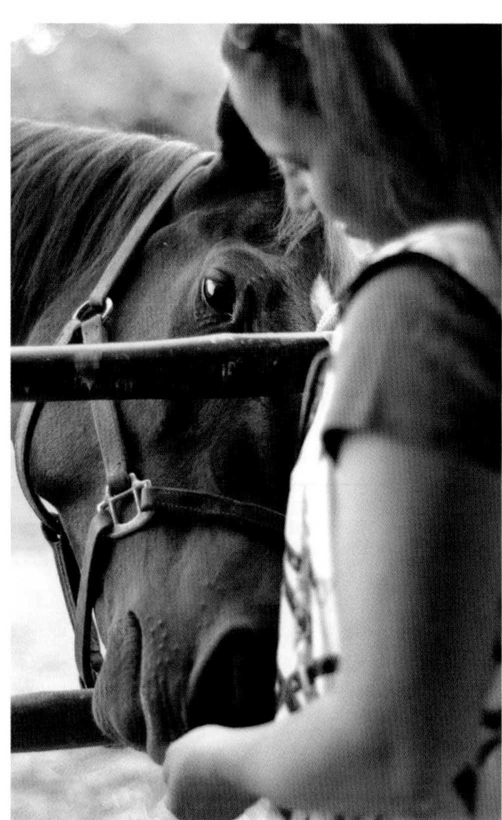

Equine Fact

Whiskers and the hair around a horse's eyes are more than decorative. They should never be trimmed, because they help the horse sense nearby objects.

BEHIND THE SIGNS

Prey Versus Predator

Nature provided the horse with the tools needed to survive in the wild, traits still in evidence in domesticated breeds. An impressive field of vision and the ability to see far into the distance, a well-developed sense of smell that allows the horse to sniff out danger, and an acute sense of hearing have all contributed to a species that has stayed ahead of predators to remain a strong presence today.

THE EXTRA SENSE

Swedish research has scientifically demonstrated what many who spend time around equines know instinctively: horses have a sixth sense that is able to pick up on lack of rider confidence. Findings from the Department of Animal Environment and Health at the University of Agricultural Sciences in Uppsala show that a nervous rider makes for a nervous horse, evidenced by the increased rider heart rate mimicked by the horse.

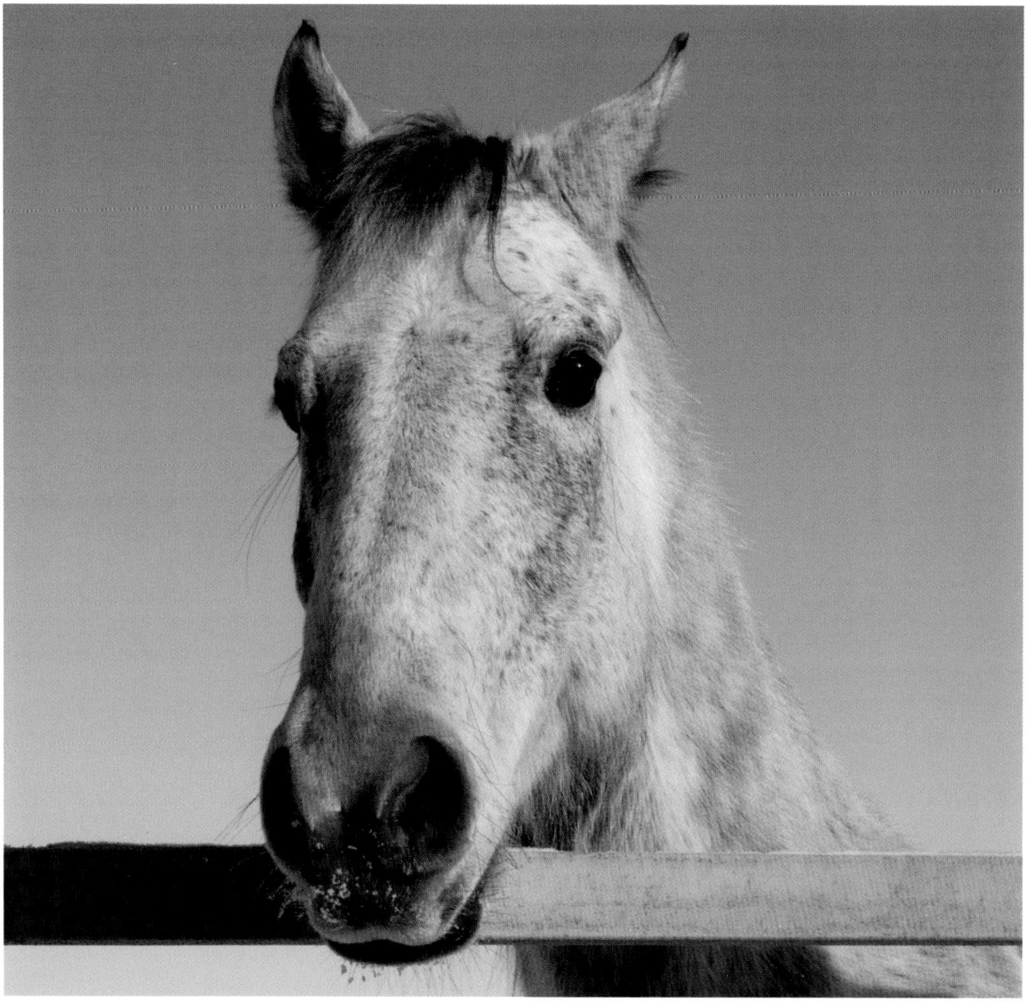

EARS AND HEARING

Horses may not understand all of the words you use, but their hearing is acute, and talking to them helps communicate that you are not a threat.

The funnel-like shape of the horse's ears contributes to their superior sense of hearing, helping to trap sound waves and send them to the ear canal. Their ears are also highly mobile, and thus better designed to capture sound. Each ear can move independently to pinpoint a sound's location, enabling equines to determine much about the sound before they see what is causing it. This mobility also means that they do not have to turn their whole body toward the noise. Instead, just their ears move toward it, so that if they need to run from danger they are ready to flee.

No.3

FIRST IMPRESSIONS

HORSE BREEDS AND TYPES

The connection between people and horses is one that can be traced through over 6,000 years. During this time the role of horses has changed, but their popularity has remained. Different breeds have played their part in the major events of history, and since domestication new breeds have been introduced.

The American Horse Council reports that there are 9.2 million horses in the United States, with 4.6 million people involved in the industry as horse owners, service providers, employees, and volunteers. Tens of millions more participate as spectators or horse enthusiasts. In Britain there are 17 horses per 1,000 people, and a total equine population of between 1 and 1.3 million, according to The British Horse Society. These numbers illustrate the enduring affinity between human and horse, and give new meaning to the term "horse power."

If you are thinking of buying a horse, it's important to understand how its breed translates to temperament and its best use. Horse ownership is a long-term commitment of time and money, and without this research you risk "putting the cart before the horse," because—although each horse is unique—breed characteristics help determine your best match in terms of your skill level and the activity you're most interested in. The sensitive and speedy Thoroughbred may not be suitable for a novice, for example, or for someone more interested in hacking than racing.

Of the over 150 breeds worldwide, some of the more well-known are listed below—a "mounting block," or starting point, to better understand breeds.

ANDALUSIAN

Named for its place of origin, this is an ancient breed descended from the Iberian horses of Spain and Portugal. Their prowess on the battlefield is well documented, with evidence suggesting that their role in the cavalry was established as early as 2000 BCE.

In contrast to their powerful and regal appearance, the temperament of the Andalusian horse is docile. Known for its intelligence and athleticism, today it is a rare breed. Andalusians are employed for pleasure riding as well as showjumping, and they excel at dressage. They stand from 15 to 16.2 hands high and are most often gray, although they may also be bay, black, dun, or palomino.

APPALOOSA

Prehistoric cave paintings and early manuscripts depict images of horses that look like the Appaloosa, but it wasn't until the 1700s that this breed gained recognition through the efforts of the Nez Perce tribe of American Indians, who selectively bred and harnessed the power of these horses for hunting. The Appaloosa horse has a unique coat pattern, with six main patterns of spotting recognized within the breed. They are also easily identifiable due to their mottled skin, white sclera—the readily visible outer membrane of the eyeball that gives the appearance of human eyes—and their striped hooves. Standing between 14.2 and 16 hands high, the Appaloosa horse is hardy and has a quiet and tractable temperament, making it a valued family horse as well as a versatile mount for Western and English disciplines.

ARABIAN

The Arabian horse appeared in rock paintings dating back to 2500 BCE and is one of the most influential breeds throughout history, with Arabian bloodlines used to improve the quality of other breeds. Developed in the Middle East, they were used as war mounts for thousands of years, with Genghis Khan, Alexander the Great, and Napoleon Bonaparte all said to favor this breed.

Known for bravery, endurance, a gentle disposition, intelligence, and high spirits, Arabians are well suited to most equine activities and sports, and excel at endurance competitions. They are generally smaller horses, standing at 14.1 to 15.1 hands, and they may be gray, chestnut, bay, or black in color. Recognized for their beauty, Arabians have small heads, large eyes, a long neck, a high tail carriage, and strong legs.

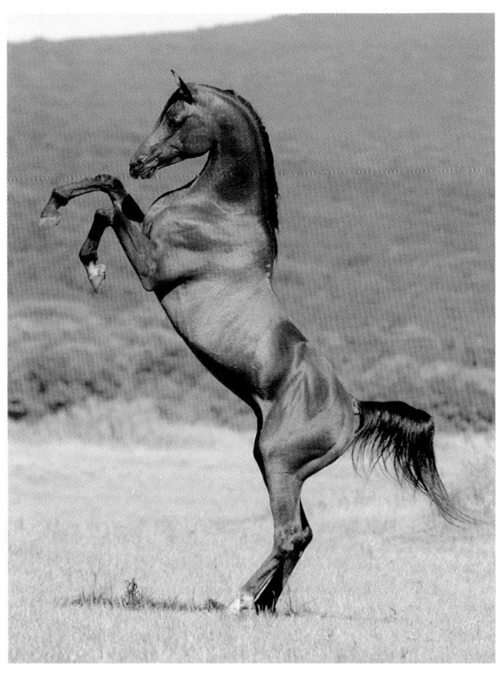

FRIESIAN

Originating in the Netherlands, the Friesian (also known as Frisian) is one of the earliest horse breeds bred in Europe. They are also an influential breed within the horse world, with many other breeds tracing ancestry back to them. Their powerful build, regal appearance, agility, and high stepping movement once made them a popular warhorse. Today those same traits make the Friesian a favorite carriage horse and dressage mount. Known as "gentle giants" due to their build and easy-going temperament, they also make a good family horse but—given their size—are not often found in endurance or eventing disciplines.

LIPIZZANER

The Lipizzaner breed can be traced back to the 16th century. Today they are most often associated with the Spanish Riding School of Vienna, where they are trained in classical dressage to perform balletlike movements, known as "airs above the ground." Given their small numbers you may not see this breed often, but they are also suited to eventing, hunting, and driving. Longevity is a common trait, as this breed matures late. Lipizzaners are born bay or black and become lighter as they age, growing into the white coat they are known for between five to eight years of age (although some adults have a brown or black coat).

MINIATURE

Favored pets of 17th-century European nobles, Miniatures also worked in the mines. The latter role led them to be imported to America, where, in the 1800s, they were an important means of transporting materials. They stand between six and seven hands high so are not a suitable mount. However, this has not detracted from their popularity as a pet—minis of all colors can also be found in competition and special events, such as driving and halter classes.

BREED ASSOCIATIONS

Breed associations are a valuable source of information. Their role is to promote their chosen breed by providing information, sponsoring shows, and maintaining a registry of horses belonging to that breed. Given that there are over 150 different breeds worldwide, there are too many associations to list here, but you will find them online.

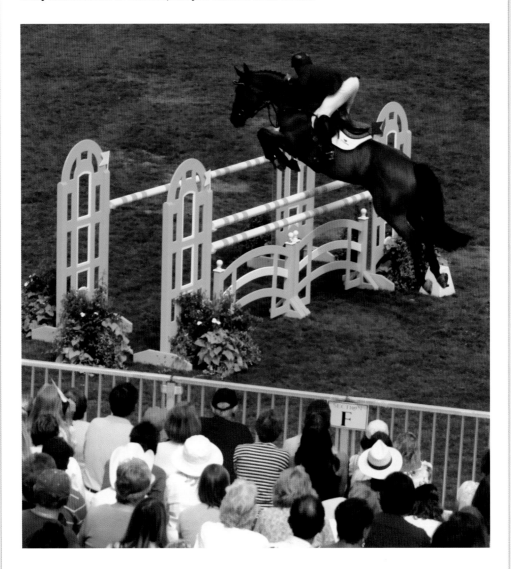

MORGAN

The Morgan dates back to the 1700s in Vermont, and is one of the oldest horse breeds developed in the United States. The story of the Morgan is one familiar to many horse-loving children due to Marguerite Henry's book about the father of the breed, known as Figure. He was a good-natured, hard-working stallion of unknown ancestry (thought to be of Arabian, Thoroughbred, or Dutch breeding), owned by a teacher named Justin Morgan. Although details from the book are disputed, it is agreed that Figure, later known by his owner's name, was the foundation sire for the Morgan breed.

Morgans are strong, industrious, eager to please, and refined in appearance—with small heads and highly arched necks. They are usually bay, black, or chestnut, but can be any solid color. They have a high-stepping action, and stand from 14.1 to 15.2 hands. Many are ridden solely for pleasure, although Morgans also excel in competition and show rings.

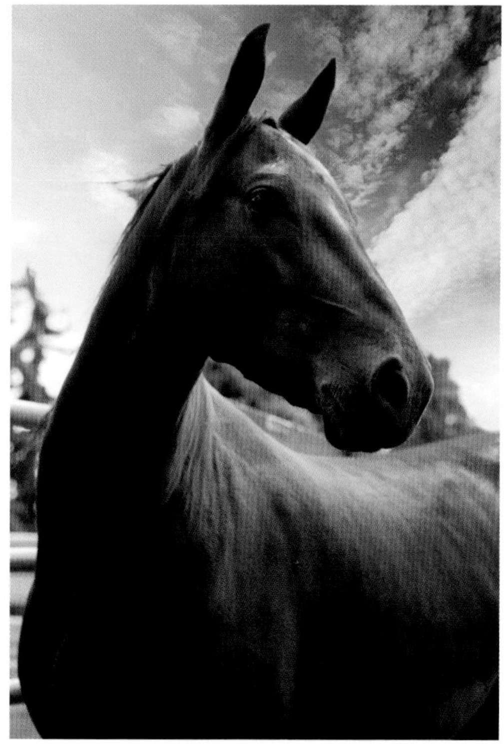

MUSTANG

Mustangs have a long and colorful history—one that saw them thundering wild and free across the American plains. Brought to America by the Spanish conquistadors, these domesticated horses were either lost or stolen and went feral. Today, untamed Mustangs continue to roam free, protected by US law.

Domesticated Mustangs are ridden on the trail, as well as in English and Western disciplines. They generally stand between 13 and 16 hands and can be found in all colors, with their variations in appearance a result of being interbred with many other horse breeds.

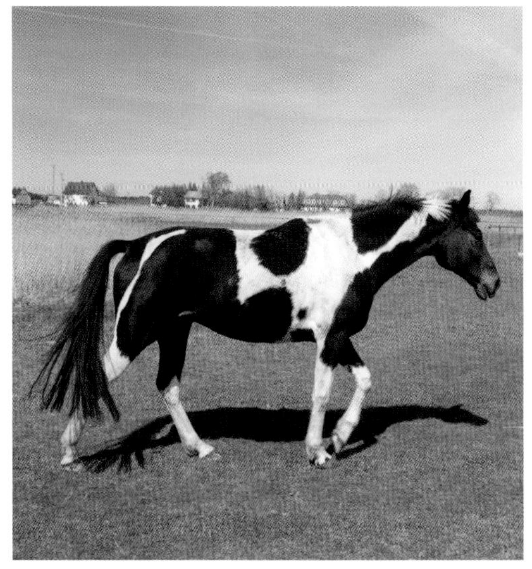

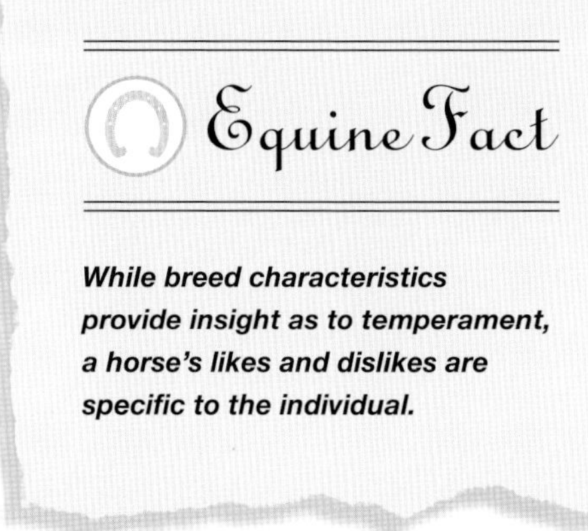

Equine Fact

While breed characteristics provide insight as to temperament, a horse's likes and dislikes are specific to the individual.

PAINT HORSE

First recognized as a breed in 1965, the Paint Horse dates back much further than that. As early as 1519, the voyage of Spanish explorer Hernando Cortés described carrying two horses with the colored coats that these horses are known for. The result of breeding between Quarter Horses, Paints are recognized by one of three coat patterns: Overo—a dark base with white irregular markings; Tobiana—a white base with dark rounded markings; or Tovero—dark pigmentation around the ears or mouth. Some have spots at the base of the tail, flank, or chest, while others may have one or both eyes blue in color. They have a gentle disposition, and a height that ranges from 15 to 16 hands. Popular in North America, they excel in Western events, but may also be seen in other riding disciplines.

PASO FINO

Originating in South America, this horse is prized for its speed and stamina, and its superior ability as a trail horse. Known for its unusual gait, the Paso Fino walks and canters but does not trot. It stands between 13.2 and 15.2 hands tall and is found in all colors.

TYPES OF BREEDS

Horses are categorized not only by breed but also by type: hotblood, warmblood, or coldblood. In general, hotbloods, such as Arabians, are known for speed and stamina and are used for racing. Warmbloods, such as the Tennessee Walking Horse and the Trakehner, are used for sport and competition, such as showjumping, combined driving, dressage, and eventing. Coldbloods, such as draft breeds like the Clydesdale, are most often used for working or hauling.

QUARTER HORSE

Horses imported from England to the American West were bred with the horses of the Chickasaw Indian, eventually developing into the Quarter Horse. Deriving its name from its ability to outrun other breeds in quarter-mile racing, this horse has a steady and easy-going nature that contributes to its popularity. Its historical use for cattle herding means that it excels in Western events, as well as other disciplines. It comes in 17 recognized colors, including the prominent brownish-red color known as sorrel. It is a compact and muscular horse, with a height range from 14.3 to 16 hands tall.

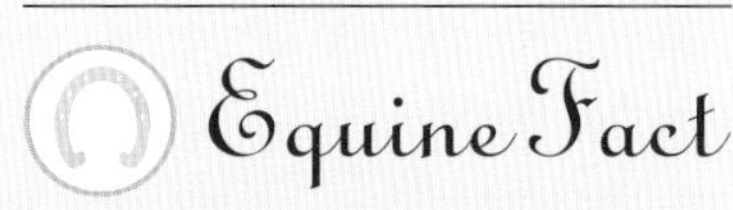

The quarter-mile race they were named for remains the most popular distance for racing Quarter Horses, with the best completing the 440 yards in 21 seconds or less.

SADDLEBRED

The Saddlebred is a gaited horse, which means that in addition to the usual walk, trot, cantor, or gallop, some of these horses can also perform what's known as the "rack" and "stepping" paces, in which the legs on each side move together. Selective breeding led to this, with the aim of making long-distance riding more comfortable. Developed in Kentucky, the Saddlebred is descended from the now extinct Narragansett Pacer, imported from England, and the Morgan. They are typically found in many colors, particularly chestnut, with height ranging from 15 to 17 hands. This graceful and athletic breed is most often used as a pleasure horse or exhibited as high-stepping show horses, either five-gaited or three-gaited. Their temperament is both eager to please and spirited.

SHETLAND PONY

Originating in Scotland, these ponies are hardy and, despite their smaller size, powerful. These characteristics came in handy in the past, when Shetland ponies cultivated land, pulled carts and carriages, or worked in the mines. Today they are one of the most popular ponies worldwide. Their compact bodies, along with their gentle and easy-going temperaments, make them a good mount for children. They are also shown in harness class, and are favored for leisure driving outside of the show ring.

Shetland ponies have long manes and tails, and thick hair, which protected them from the harsh climate of the islands they were named for. They range in size, with an official maximum height of 42 inches (10.2 hands) in the UK and 46 inches (11.2 hands) in the United States. Interestingly, they are known as the strongest equine, relative to size.

BEHIND THE SIGNS

Making the Grade

Purebred horses may get more attention, but horses whose parentage is not known—and therefore cannot be classified within a breed group—make wonderful companion horses. Known as "grade horses," they may not follow any breed conformation but are no less lovable. Breed is only indicative of temperament and ability. What really matters is the horse's health and personality—two very important aspects that breed may influence, but are the direct result of the care and handling the horse is given.

TENNESSEE WALKING HORSE

It was developed in Tennessee and is known for its smooth gait, which makes it a comfortable horse to ride for extended periods. This horse stands from 15 to 16 hands tall and can be found in bay, black, chestnut, sorrel, and white. The Tennessee Walker is shown in both English and Western disciplines, as well as being a popular choice for leisure riding.

Equine Fact

Crossbred horses are the offspring of two different breeds. Breeders may intentionally crossbreed so that the offspring carries desirable traits from both parents.

BEHIND THE SIGNS

Horse Power

Thoroughbreds are the fastest horses in the world at long-distance racing, and can reach speeds of approximately 40 mph (64 kph) on the racetrack, depending on the individual horse. Although most frequently associated with racing—either as distance runners or sprinters—they also excel at showjumping, polo, hunting, and dressage. The Quarter Horse is typically faster at shorter distances, with some reaching over 50 mph (80.5 kph). They are bred for sprinting, and are also commonly found in the show ring competing in Western riding events.

THOROUGHBRED

The Thoroughbred originated in England in the 1700s and has since impacted greatly the equine world, with its bloodline contributing to many other breeds. Bred for agility, they are primarily racehorses, although their skills extend to the show ring and three-day eventing. They can be bold and temperamental, so are often best suited to more experienced riders.

Thoroughbreds are aristocratic in appearance, yet much tougher than they look. They are lean and lanky, standing from 14.2 to 17 hands tall, and are most often bay, chestnut, brown, black, or gray in color.

TRAKEHNER

This breed is more than 400 years old, and is one of the earliest European warmbloods. Its name has been shortened over time, from "the East Prussian Warmblood Horse of Trakehner Origin," after the location where it was first bred. They are considered a lighter and more refined warmblood, reflecting their thoroughbred ancestry.

Despite their large size, the Trakehner are elegant, and are known for their "floating trot." Athletic and intelligent, they compete in many disciplines, and are very popular as dressage and eventing mounts. They can be found in all solid colors, and stand from 15.2 to 17 hands.

WELSH COB

Established in the 15th century in Wales, this breed served as mounts for British knights. Since then, the Welsh Cob (also known as the Welsh Section D Pony) has continued to work as a cavalry horse, as well as being a valued farm animal—in both cases they prove excellent on rugged terrain. Today the traits that made the Welsh Cob such a popular choice for so long—its strength, agility, and tractability—are most frequently used in hunting, jumping, and driving, among other disciplines. They stand from 13.2 hands tall and come in all colors except pinto (or colored) patterns, such as piebald and skewbald.

No. 4

THE LANGUAGE OF HORSE OWNERS

DESCRIBING HORSES CORRECTLY

Horse owners have a lingo all their own. It may sound like a foreign language to the uninitiated, but it's an easy language to learn—and one that is necessary in order to communicate correctly in the equine world.

It's common for enthusiasts of a particular pursuit to share a specialized vocabulary, whether it is in relation to cooking, music, or—in this case—horses. To describe a horse there are specific terms used for age and gender, color and markings, breed (see chapter 3), and height.

AGE AND GENDER

Age really is just a number when it comes to competition horses. These horses are considered a year older each January 1 in the northern hemisphere, and each August 1 in the southern hemisphere. For example, a foal (a horse that is under the age of one) that is born on December 1 would be classed as a yearling (a horse between one and two years old) as of January 1. However, according to the calendar date of birth, this horse is only one month old.

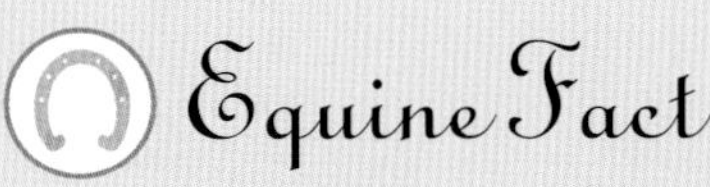

Most domestic horses live for between 25 and 30 years.

Endurance riding is an exception to the rule. In this discipline, the horse's actual calendar date of birth is used.

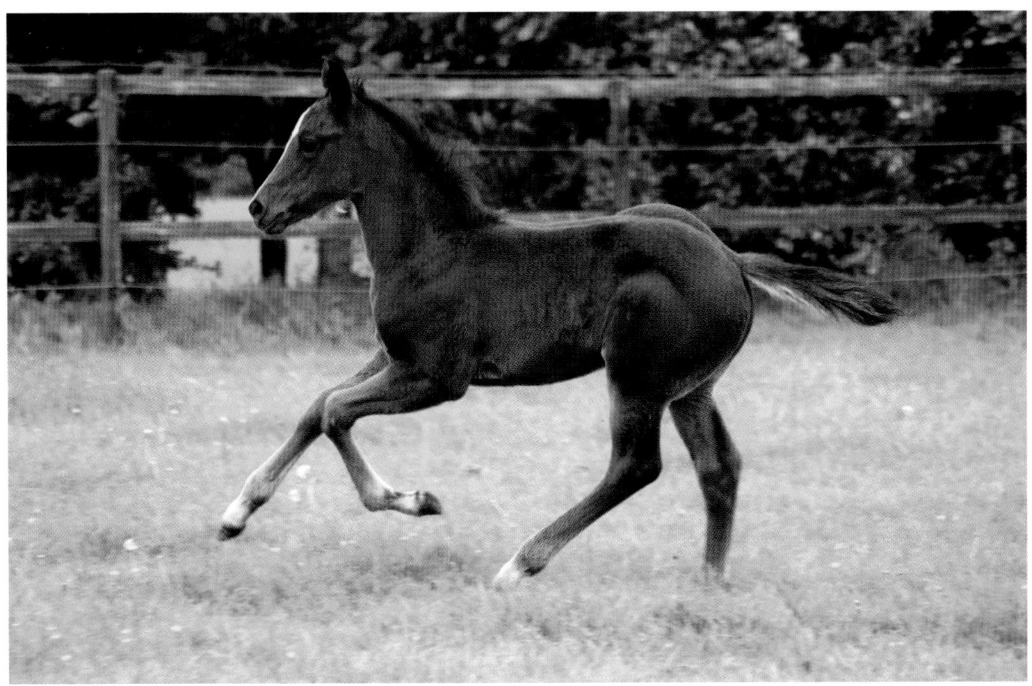

TERMINOLOGY: AGE AND GENDER

1. Foal: A young male or female horse under the age of one. A male foal may be known as a "colt foal," and a female foal may be known as a "filly foal."

2. Yearling: A young male or female between one and two years old. A male that has not been castrated may be known as a "yearling colt," and a female may be known as a "yearling filly."

3. Colt: A young male under the age of four.

4. Filly: A young female under the age of four.

5. Stallion: An adult male over four years old that has not been castrated.

6. Mare: An adult female at four years or older.

7. Gelding: A castrated male of any age.

The definitions may vary slightly depending on organization, discipline, or country. For example, in harness racing a mare is a female horse more than three years old, while in other disciplines a mare may refer to a female horse over four years of age. In thoroughbred racing, colts and fillies are younger than five years old in the UK, or under four years old in Australia. The terms "stallion" and "horse" are sometimes used interchangeably.

1

2

3

4

5

6

7

TERMINOLOGY: COLOR

1. Bay: The coat can vary from pale to dark brown. The mane and tail are black, and lower legs may also be black.

2. Black: A solid black coat, mane, and tail.

3. Brown: A dark brown or light black coat, with a black mane and tail. The shank, muzzle, and inside upper legs may be slightly lighter in color.

4. Buckskin: A yellow or gold body coloration, with a black mane and tail. The lower legs are usually black and may have white markings.

5. Chestnut: A light or dark brownish, red coat, mane, and tail.

6. Cremello: A cream-colored coat that may be off-white or a pale gold, with a white mane and tail. Sometimes referred to as "double dilutes" because they received two copies of the same dilute gene necessary for that coat color.

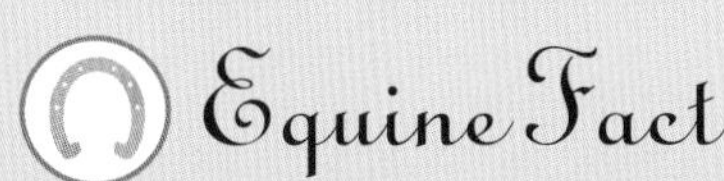

Nature provided horses with coat colors as a means of camouflage, to help protect equines from predators.

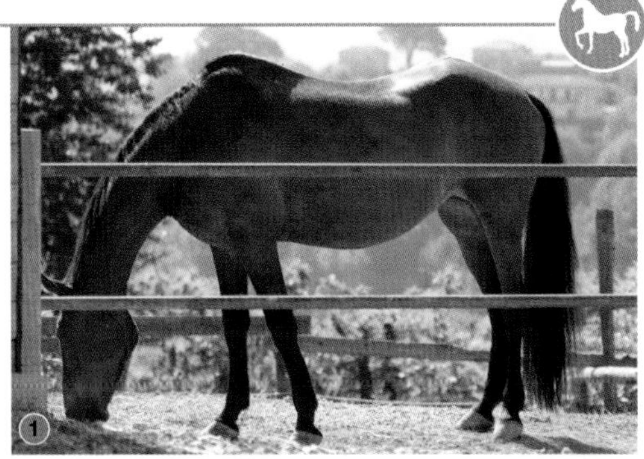

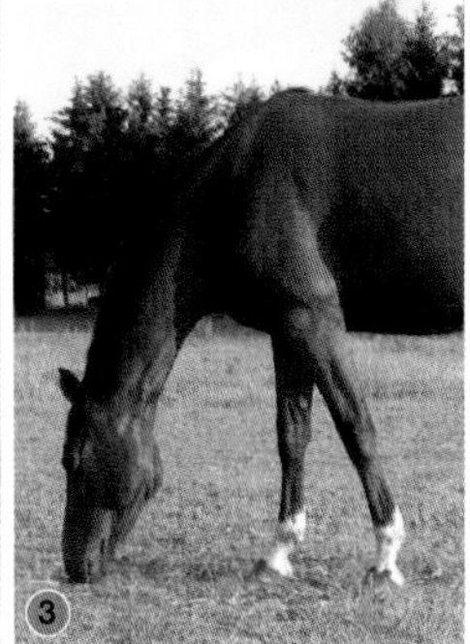

7. Dun: A pale or rich gold body color, with a black or brown mane and tail. These horses will also have a black stripe running down their back. "Red duns" have a reddish tint to their coat, with a red or blonde mane and tail.

8. Gray: This may refer to a variety of shades, from almost white to dark gray. These horses are usually born solid-colored (brown or black, for example), with their coat lightening as they mature.

9. Grulla: Also known as Grullo, this is a dark, slate-colored coat (in brown or gray shades), with a black mane and tail. There may also be a dark stripe running down the back, as well as dark legs.

10. Palomino: A pale or rich golden-yellow body coloration, with a mane and tail that is white.

11. Piebald: Also known as Colored, or Pinto, this refers to a black and white coat. The amount of each color and its patterning varies. The mane and tail will be black, white, or contain both colors.

12. Roan: This coat pattern can be any color, with white hairs ticked through the coat. A "blue roan" will have a base color of black that, with the white hairs, gives its coat a bluish or gray appearance. A "red" or "strawberry roan" will have a chestnut base coat, mixed with white hairs.

13. Skewbald: Also known as Colored, or Pinto, the coat may be a combination of white and any color other than black. The amount of each color and its patterning varies.

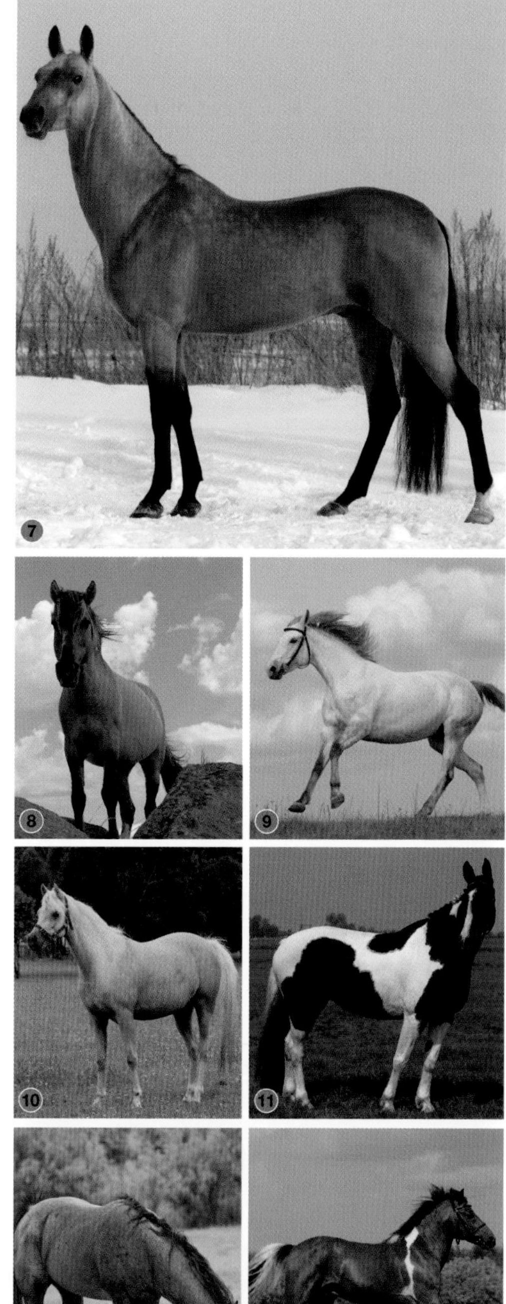

TERMINOLOGY: FACIAL MARKINGS

1. Bald: A white stripe that runs down the middle of the face from forehead to muzzle. The stripe is wide, extending out from the center of the face to the sides.

2. Blaze: A white stripe that runs down the middle of the face, along the bridge of the nose. It differs from "bald" in that the stripe is not as wide.

3. Snip: A white spot on the muzzle between the nostrils or just below them.

4. Star: A white marking on the forehead or between the eyes.

5. Stripe (also called Strip): A narrow white stripe on the bridge of the nose or the center of the face.

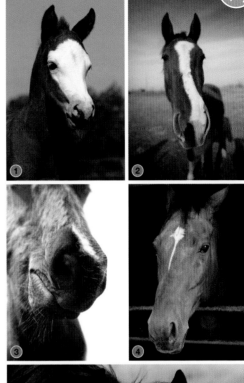

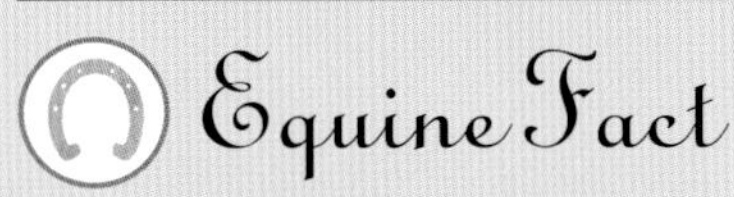

A horse can have multiple facial markings and various leg markings.

TERMINOLOGY: LEG MARKINGS

1. Coronet: A narrow white band just above the hoof.

2. Fetlock or Sock (sometimes called Boot): A white marking that starts just above the hoof and extends past the ankle (fetlock) but not as far as the knee (hock).

3. Half Cannon: A white marking that starts just above the hoof and extends halfway up the leg.

4. Pastern: A white marking that starts just above the hoof but stops below the ankle (fetlock).

5. Stocking: A white marking that starts just above the hoof and extends to the knee (hock).

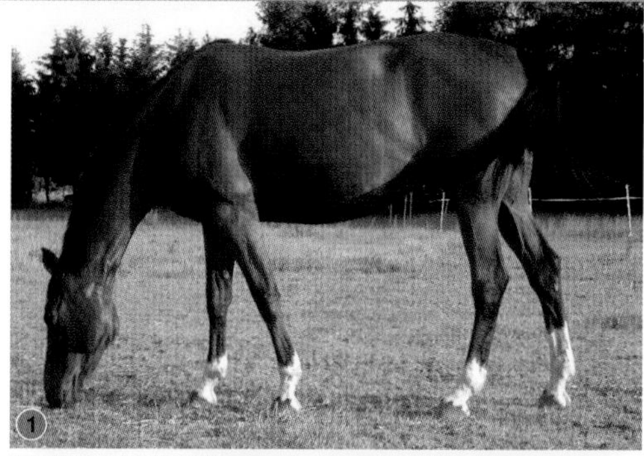

1

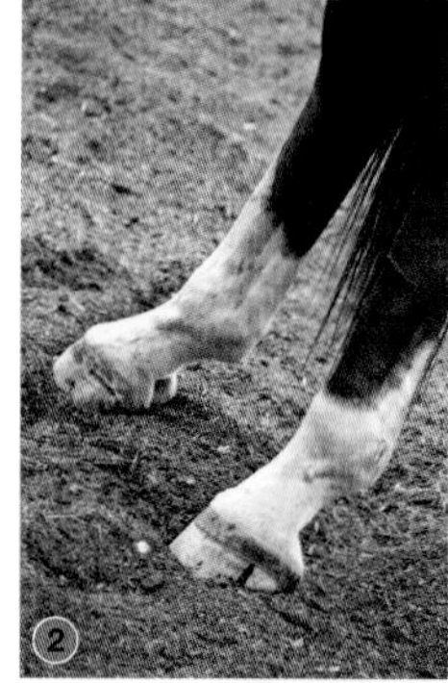

2

3

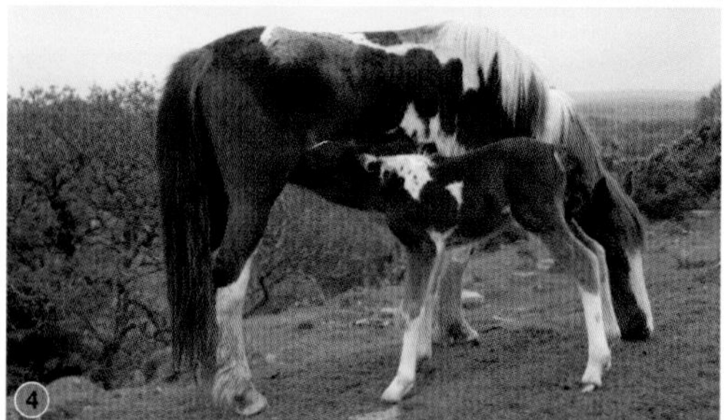

4

5

USE THE LINGO: SAMPLE SENTENCES

Here are a few examples of how the terminology might be applied within a sentence.

- That black and white Pinto is a beautiful horse. (US)
- That Piebald is a beautiful horse. (UK)
- Even with regular grooming, it's difficult to keep my horse's half cannon white.
- Horse for sale: Black in color, with four matching stockings and a perfect blaze.
- Acapella is a 15-year-old dappled gray Arabian mare, who is 15.2 hands with no face or leg markings.

TERMINOLOGY: HEIGHT

A horse's height is described in hands. One hand equals four inches (10.16 cm). Therefore, a horse that is 15.1 hands tall is 61 inches (155 cm). This may be abbreviated to 15.1 h or 15.1 hh—both have the same meaning, with "h" standing for "hands," and "hh" the abbreviation for "hands high."

To measure a horse's height you can use a regular tape measure or a specialty horse measuring tape or pole. The latter shows the measurement in hands, so there is no need to convert it from inches or centimeters.

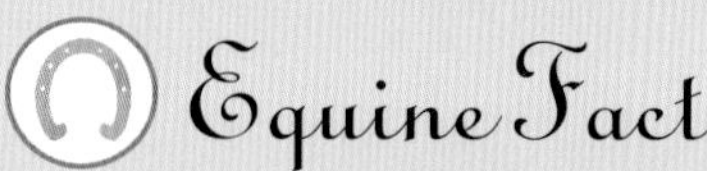

The size of horses varies by breed. Riding horses are generally between 14 and 17 hands tall. Draft horses are typically between 16 and 18 hands tall.

To calculate its height, a horse is measured from the ground to the highest point of his withers (the highest part of a horse's back, located just where his back joins the neck).

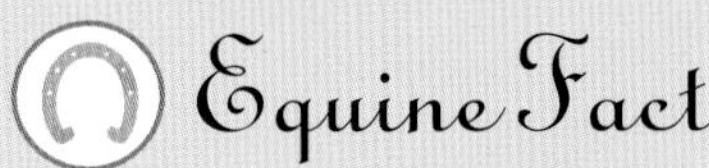

Equine Fact

The use of hands as a measurement unit came from the days when devices like tape measures were not available or commonly used. Hands were a convenient measure and, as the tradition continued, it was standardized over time.

BEHIND THE SIGNS

How Many Hands?

To say that your horse is 15.4 hands tall would be incorrect. Each hand is four inches, so the correct height description for your horse would be 16 hands. Another common mistake is to record 15.5 h for a horse that measures 15 and a half hands. Since each hand is four inches, that would make half of a hand two inches. So, in this case, the correct way to note the horse's height would be 15.2 h (although, just to make it more confusing, when said aloud it may be described as 15 and a half). Make sense? Don't worry, you will quickly become familiar with this most traditional of measurements.

No. 5

EQUINE COMMUNICATION 1

VOCAL EXPRESSION

***A** happy horse is generally a quiet horse, although foals and mares may be more vocal. As a result, the spoken language of equines is small on vocabulary but large on nuance. One word, or vocalization, manages to "say" many different things, depending on the accompanying body language (see chapter 6).*

The language of the horse is universal. Regardless of their location in the world, they all use the same sounds to communicate a variety of messages, from parental concern to mating interest. Their main vocabulary consists of the nicker, neigh, snort, blow, squeal, and scream. When you are able to translate the meaning behind these sounds, you will better understand your horse.

THE NICKER

WHAT YOU HEAR:
A soft vibrating sound, or a louder, more energetic vibrating noise.

WHAT IT MEANS:
The soft nicker:
"Hi, nice to see you," or *"Come closer."*
This gentle nicker is an affectionate greeting. It's often used in parenthood, for example, by the mare to her foal. It may be used by a horse to show affection to a herdmate, or to a person he likes, particularly someone who feeds him regularly. It will often be accompanied by a gentle nudge from the horse's nose.

The louder, more energetic nicker:
"Hey gorgeous!"
The louder nicker is a mating call, used by a stallion when courting a mare. It's often accompanied by head shaking. In both versions of the nicker the horse's mouth will be closed and he will look alert, with his ears pricked to the person or animal of interest.

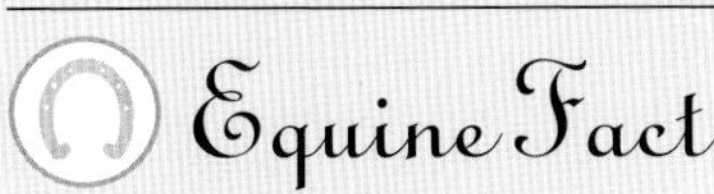

Equine Fact

Unlike dogs, who bark and yelp, horses do not vocalize pain very clearly (see chapters 16 and 17).

BEHIND THE SIGNS

The Fearful Nicker

As when interpreting any vocal expression, look to the whole picture, not just the sound, since similar sounds can communicate very different messages. Typically, the nicker is a positive sound, but on occasion it may be apprehensive and unsure. The fearful nicker is accompanied by ears that move back and forth repeatedly. The horse will pace, his eyes may roll, and his breathing may be rapid. If this is the message then the translation is "I don't like this," or "What's going on?" This horse is frightened, so it's best to remove him from whatever situation has caused his unease. This may also be a good time for grooming, which should help to relax the horse.

THE NEIGH (OR WHINNY)

WHAT YOU HEAR:
A high-pitched squeal, which turns into the nicker and repeats.

WHAT IT MEANS:
The anxious neigh: *"Where is everybody?"*
The answering neigh: *"I'm here."*
Horses are most likely to vocalize when separated from others, often using the "neigh" in these situations. This is the sound of a horse on his own, wondering where his herd is, or missing a particular friend. His eyes will flick back and forth; his tail will lift and lower repeatedly, or be tucked between his legs; and he may pace repeatedly.

The expectant, confident neigh:
"Where is everybody? Feed me, now!"
This is accompanied by forward-pricked ears, and a slightly shifted tail. The neigh is the loudest and longest of horse sounds, which makes sense as it's most often used to send a message to those who aren't nearby. It can communicate anxiety and loneliness, or send a message about feeding time, depending on the body language used.

THE SNORT

WHAT YOU HEAR:
A loud and rapid exhalation of air from the nostrils.

WHAT IT MEANS:
"Is this dangerous?"
The snort is very brief, but also very loud. The horse's body will be tense and his head will be outstretched, with his gaze focused intently on the object that has caught his interest. If the horse decides that *"Yes, this object is dangerous,"* he will startle and move away from it. If he decides *"Everything is fine,"* he will then relax.

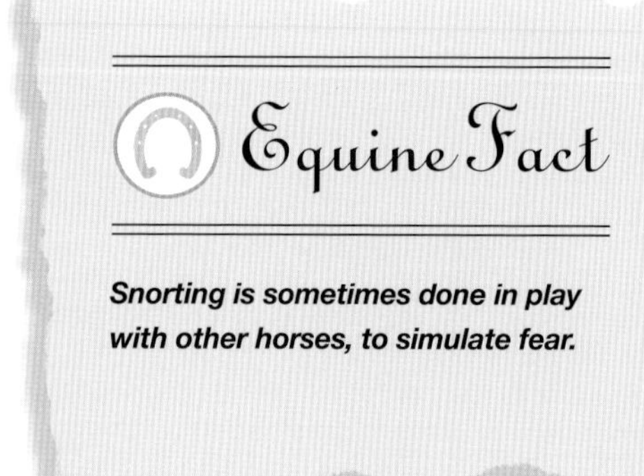

Equine Fact

Snorting is sometimes done in play with other horses, to simulate fear.

THE BLOW

WHAT YOU HEAR:
An exhalation of air through the nose, with the lips closed. It is much like the snort, but without the vibrating, fluttering sound.

WHAT IT MEANS:
"Are you friend or foe?"
When two horses meet face to face they will blow on each other. A gentle blowing, perhaps accompanied by nuzzling, is the friendly response. If the blowing is followed by any signs of aggression, such as squealing, stomping, or nipping, then the answer to the question is an emphatic "Stay away, I'm not your friend!" Like all vocalizations, there can be multiple meanings. To decipher what your horse is saying, look to the accompanying behavior.

If a horse is curious or unsure about an object, he may blow on it, in the same way he blows on another horse to find out if he is friendly or not. If the horse decides the object he's focused on is not a threat, he'll relax. If he feels it is dangerous he will tense up, and may spook. Objects that cause horses to spook are things that are unfamiliar to them. Some of these are everyday items, such as balloons, flags, and plastic shopping bags blowing in the wind.

THE SQUEAL

WHAT YOU HEAR:
A high-pitched exclamation, which may be short or longer in duration, depending on the message.

WHAT IT MEANS:
"This is a warning, stay away!"
During a show of dominance between two horses the squeal will be used aggressively, to communicate to the other horse that he should *"back up, or else."*
"I don't want to!"
The horse squeals while moving away from the object he is being pushed toward, for example, a trailer.

THE SCREAM

WHAT YOU HEAR:
A loud roar of anger, accompanied by aggressive body language, such as kicking and biting.

WHAT IT MEANS:
"You'll regret that!"
This is a scream full of anger and aggression. Luckily, it's rare for two horses to fight to this extent, so it is rarely heard. When intense fights do happen they will generally continue until one horse backs down, usually in flight with his tail set low.

No. 6

EQUINE COMMUNICATION 2

BODY LANGUAGE

The primary way that horses communicate is through their body language: posture, gesture, and expression. Learn to interpret it and a whole new world of communication and understanding opens up. You'll know when your horse is relaxed, excited, frustrated, or fearful, and with this knowledge comes increased confidence—in you from your horse, as well as in your own skills as a rider.

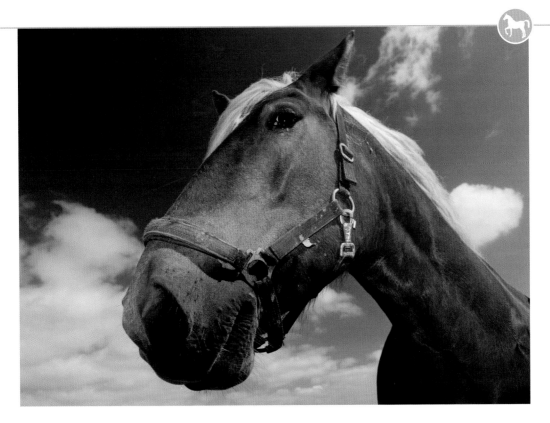

An understanding of equine body language is critical to horse–human interaction. It can help prevent accidents and also to build your bond. A horse's mood is best interpreted by looking at his body language as a whole. His head, neck, ears, eyes, muzzle, tail, and legs all communicate a message. His behaviors, postures, and expressions all have meaning. The more time you spend with your horse the better you'll become at translating his language.

HEAD AND NECK

A high head and neck position often means an agitated state: defiant, angry, or fearful. Conversely, when the head and neck are set low this usually means the horse is relaxed. He's comfortable grazing and feels safe enough to lower his head, unconcerned about predators. A level head and neck position indicates that the horse is focused and attentive to whatever is holding his gaze.

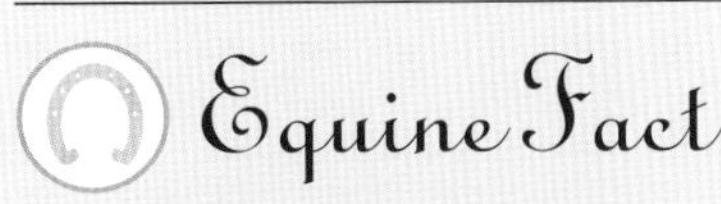

When translating horse vocabulary, look at the various behaviors, positions, and expressions that come together to form a "sentence."

THE LANGUAGE OF EARS

A horse's ears provide great insight into his mood. For example, if your horse's ears point stiffly to another horse you'll know that horse has captured his attention and there is the possibility of trouble. Lead your horse away. While hacking, or trail riding, your horse's ears may point forward, showing his attention lies with the trail and his surroundings. That's usually not a problem, unless you have specific cues you need him to pay attention to. In that case, you may want to stop and start a few times. This will help prevent him from getting too caught up in his surroundings and remind him to follow your cues.

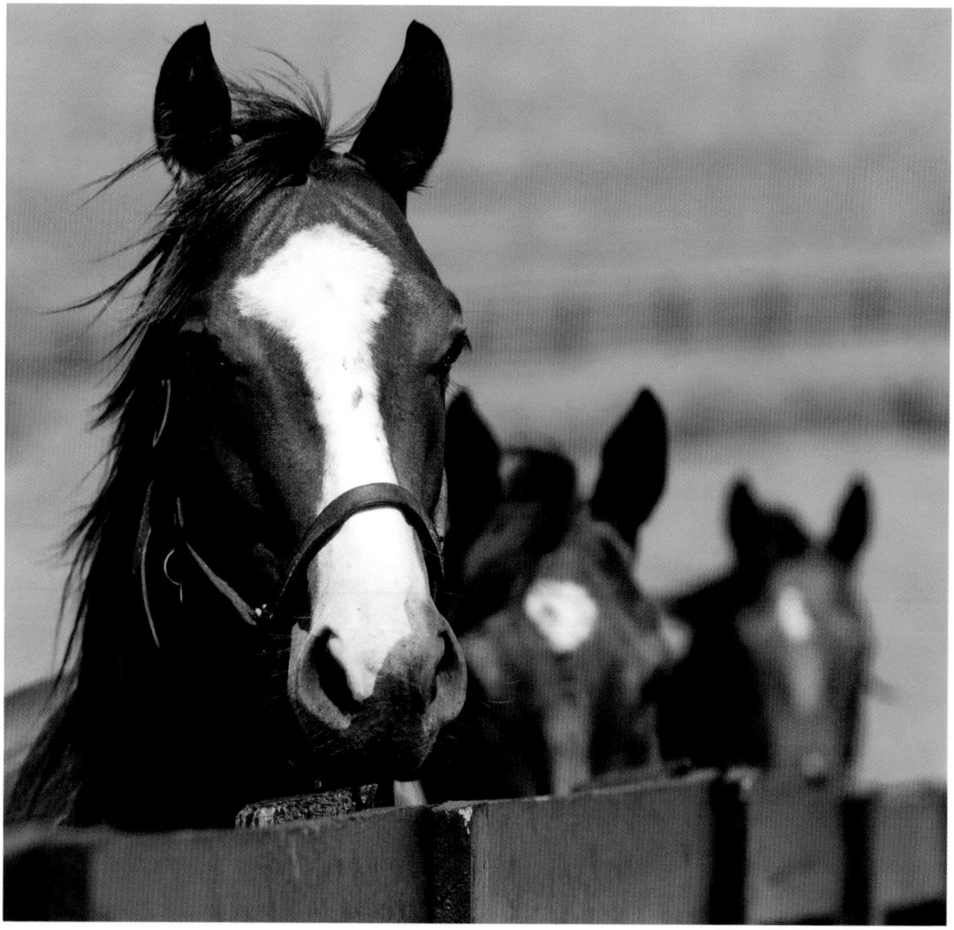

EARS

A horse's ears are a form of equine antenna, constantly transmitting information. They will point forward, back, or even to the sides, depending on his mood. His most mobile feature, they are able to communicate a great deal. When a horse's ears are pointed forward in a relaxed manner this reflects his mood: easy-going. If they are stiffly pointed forward, however, consider this a warning notice that your horse is aroused and has yet to decide whether he is looking at a threat or a treat. He may also be feeling playful and may nip as a result.

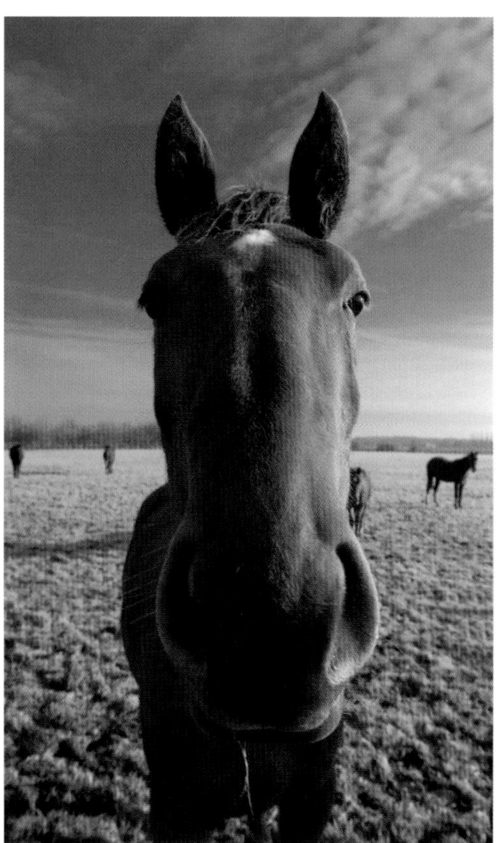

Ears that are rigidly pointing back are a definite warning. This horse is fearful or angry, and aggression may be the result. Don't mistake this for ears that are pointed back in a relaxed manner. In the latter case, the horse's ears point to where his attention is, perhaps at you while riding or grooming him. A horse's ears will swivel, and their direction shows where his interest lies in that given moment, while the stiffness of the ears expresses mood.

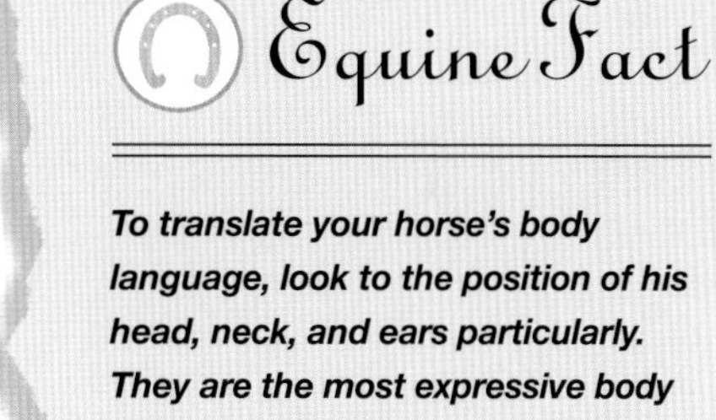

Equine Fact

To translate your horse's body language, look to the position of his head, neck, and ears particularly. They are the most expressive body parts, but his eyes, muzzle, tail, and legs also contribute to tell his story.

BEHIND THE SIGNS

Play or Aggression?

Play bites are common from young horses, especially colts. Horses explore their environments with their mouth, and this may result in them nipping at you (or at your pockets, looking for treats). To nip the nipping or biting behavior in the bud, look at when it occurs. Does your horse expect something from the behavior? Never respond with positive attention or a treat or you will be reinforcing the behavior. Is he overexcited? Lunge him to work off the excess energy. Is it aggression? If accompanied by pinned ears, for example, it's best to enlist professional help to successfully stop this behavior from the start.

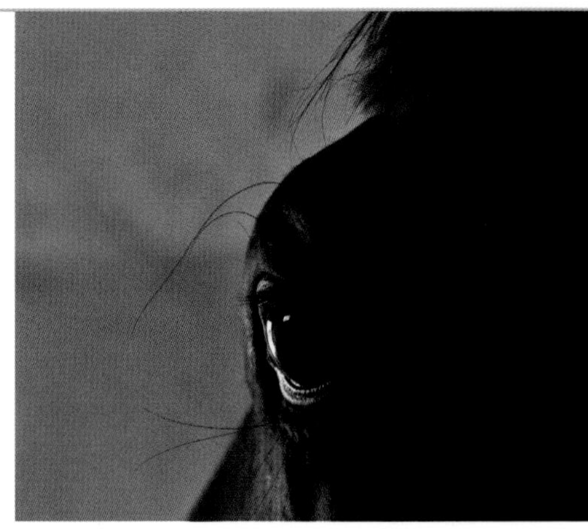

EYES

As a prey animal, the horse is very sensitive to any movement. His large eyes may communicate less, but they carefully take in all around him and work in tandem with the rest of his body to express how he's feeling. Wide eyes can indicate fear and the possibility of flight. A horse who shows the whites of his eyes (except the Appaloosa breed) is sending a definite message of aggression.

MUZZLE

Nose and mouth positioning also indicate the horse's mood, with a long nose and tight lip indications of anxiety, frustration, or impatience. It's really not that different from the expression that people use when feeling the same emotions. In the horse's case he may be communicating that he doesn't understand what is expected of him in a training session, or perhaps that his girth has been tightened too much.

An aggressive horse may bare his teeth in warning, while a relaxed horse may chew his lip slightly, in an absent-minded fashion. Opening and closing the mouth repeatedly, known as "snapping," is most often seen in young horses. It's an appeasement gesture, which translated says, "Don't be mad, I'm just a baby."

THE LANGUAGE SCALE

Who are the animal world's communication kings? Primates are near the top, with most experts agreeing that Diana monkeys would be worthy of a crown. Dogs are also a contender. But, like beauty, most argue that the answer may be in the eye of the beholder. This is because studies have yet to take into account all of the many variables that affect results. A crucial element is the familiarity between human and animal, which affects how well the animal understands our language, and how well we're able to understand their natural way of communicating. Is it based on vocal communication solely or body language as well? Just as in human linguistic systems, an extensive vocabulary doesn't always translate to more meaningful communication. Birds and cats may vocalize more than horses do, for example, but that doesn't mean the messages they communicate through sound are more extensive or detailed.

TAIL

The tail carriage of a horse varies by breed. Some, like the Arabian, naturally carry their tails held high so, although the tail can communicate mood, it's important to keep in mind that the following are generalities. Like all individual indicators, it's best to view them together to get the most accurate translation of what your horse's body language is saying.

A flagged tail can usually be interpreted as excited or playful, with a low tail indicating submissiveness. If a horse's tail is clamped down this is generally a sign of fear, and if his tail is held high it indicates alertness. An occasionally swishing tail held low indicates the horse is relaxed. A fiercely swishing tail, often seen in horses reluctant to work, says the opposite. In the latter case this horse is "wringing," indicating discomfort or annoyance (and possibly that there are too many flies around!).

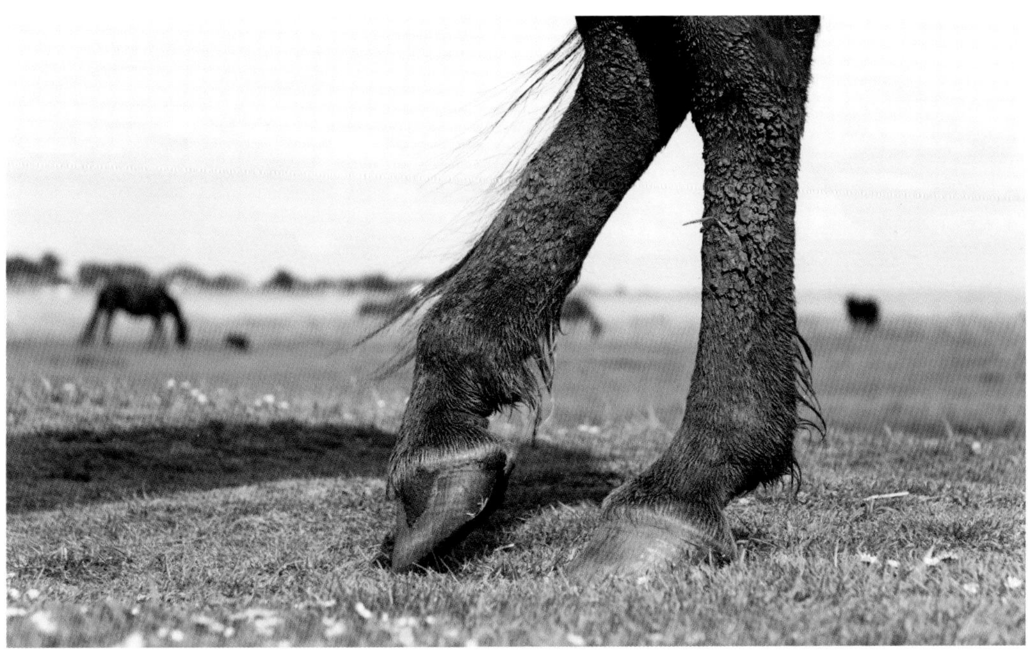

LEGS

A horse's legs can send a message that is quite obvious, such as pawing legs to show frustration, or stamping legs to communicate irritation (often a result of those pesky flies). Standing squarely on all fours indicates attention, while a dancing motion most often means nervousness or excitement. A hind leg lifted says "watch out" and is threatening, while a hind foot resting translates to relaxation.

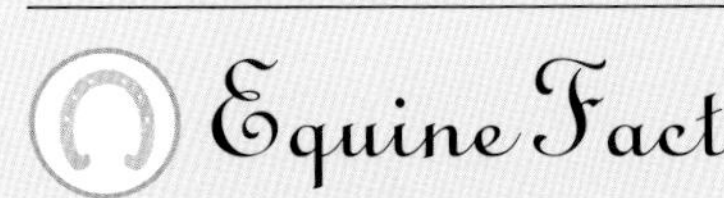

Equine Fact

Body language in humans may be less sophisticated than our equine friends, given that we rely much more on vocal communication.

Watch for anything unusual that may indicate a medical problem. Only touching the ground with a front toe, or resting the front legs may be signs of discomfort and should be investigated further.

THE BIG PICTURE

A horse's emotions are best interpreted by looking at everything together: his head and neck, ears, eyes, muzzle, tail, legs, and the context. The more time you spend with horses the better you'll become at translating their language with increased accuracy.

ALERT AND READY TO FLEE

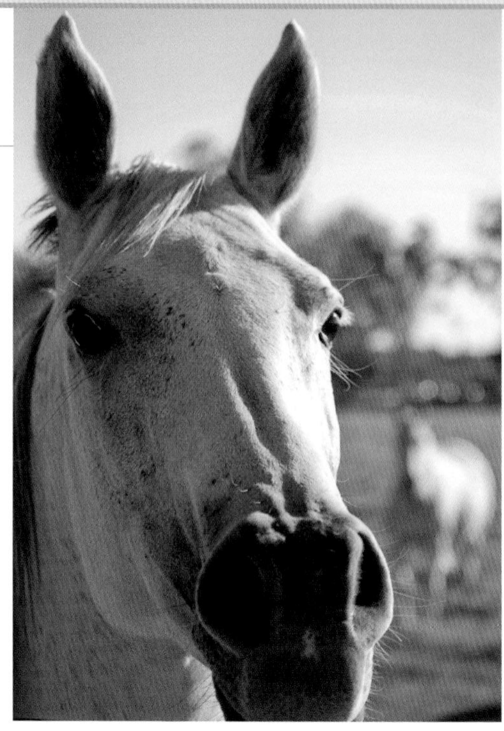

This is perhaps the most familiar body language. In this scenario the horse's head and neck will be high, his ears will be pricked, his eyes will be wide, and his nostrils will be flared.

This horse is not yet sure if there is a threat, but may not wait to find out. Something has alerted him to possible danger, and he may choose to get away whether it is real or not. This may be easier when you are not riding, as horses are less fearful when being led. But if you are riding, the same goes. If you are holding the reins correctly and are seated properly in the saddle you can react quickly.

BORED OR SLEEPY

The horse's ears will tip back and slightly to the side. His lip may also look like it is drooping, and his eyes will usually be half closed. If you see this as you approach your horse, speak to him in order to wake him up a little and get his attention.

If you are grooming your horse, speak to him throughout and keep one hand on him as you move around him, to remind him that you are there so that you don't startle him (which could result in a kick) if he has become too relaxed. If you are on the trail, you may want to cue him to start and stop a few times, to remind him to pay attention to you, rather than getting lulled by his surroundings.

DISTRACTED

The horse's ears will point in two different directions, indicating he's receiving signals from both locations, and has yet to focus on only one. This is not to be confused with when a horse points one ear in your direction at your approach or he hears the sound of your voice. In this case, depending on his other body language, he may just be relaxed and is taking note of you.

If other horses or too much activity are distracting him when you need his undivided attention, you may want to move to a quieter location.

CONTENTED

The horse's ears will point behind him, but will not be stiff or flattened to his head. His head will be slightly bent and most of his weight will be distributed over three legs, resting the fourth. His eyes will be soft and his mouth will be closed.

You will most often see this when a horse is in pasture with plenty of time to graze and act as equines should, and perhaps when he is being groomed after a long exercise session.

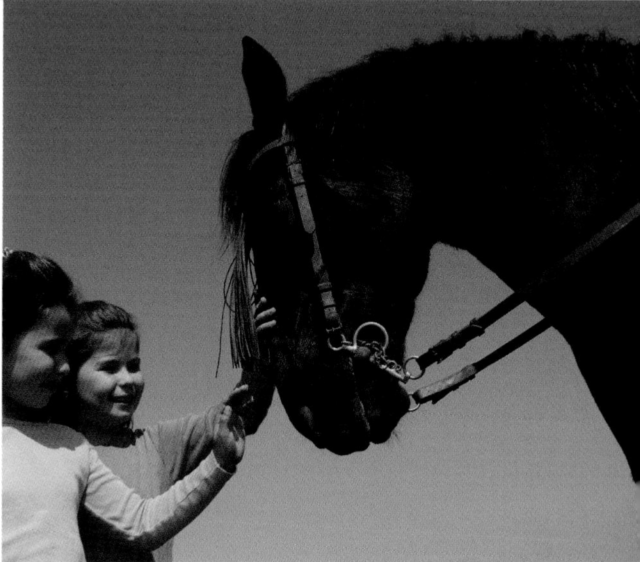

SCARED OR AGGRESSIVE

The horse's ears will be forward or flattened and back. They are also rigid—an important indication that all is not well. Combined with lips set tightly and a tense body, this generally translates as a horse that is anxious and tense. If the whites of his eyes are also showing (except in the Appaloosa breed) this is often a sign that a kick or a bite may follow, depending on the level of irritation and the horse's temperament.

BEHIND THE SIGNS

Running Machine

As prey animals, horses have been equipped with speed to help them escape predators. Speed varies from horse to horse, but in general a horse will walk at 3–4 mph (5–6 kph), trot at 8–10 mph (13–16 kph), canter at 10–17 mph (16–27 kph), and gallop at about 30 mph (48 kph). Speed is influenced by breed, stride length, build, age, condition, and athletic ability. Depending on these factors, horses may be slower or faster, with some Quarter Horses, for example, clocked at 50 mph (80 kph) in short bursts. Even foals will trot and canter hours after their birth, and gallop within their first 24 hours.

CURIOUS

Generally speaking, the direction in which a horse's ears point indicates where his attention lies. This can help you establish what is preoccupying him. It may be you, his feed, or the trail you're riding. He will usually be balanced evenly on all legs and, depending on his level of attention, his tail may be held high (very alert) or it may be held lower and gently swishing (relaxed but attentive). If your horse's eyes are also blinking more than usual he is probably thinking and processing information.

Reminder: Be careful not to misread the signs. The way your horse holds his ears is also indicative of his feelings. For example, if they are pinned rigidly forward or back this indicates fear or aggression. When relaxed, they can be a sign of where his attention is.

UNWELL

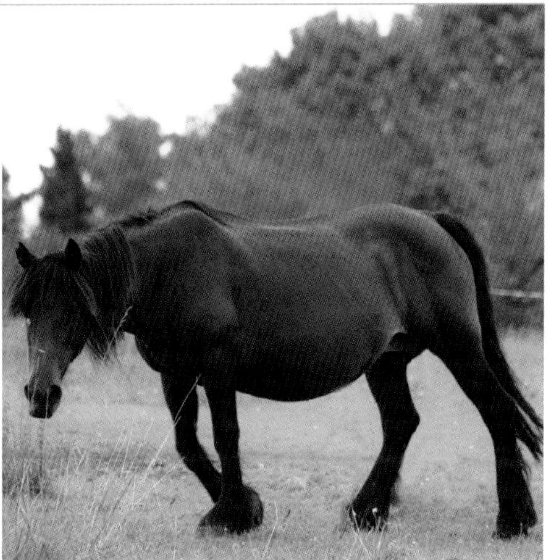

The horse's ears may be in an "airplane" position. Each ear droops slightly out to the side, reminiscent of an airplane's wings. He may be resting his front legs. Anything that is unusual for your horse can also indicate a problem.

Has his appetite, activity level, or attitude changed? Horses don't vocalize pain or injury because in the wild their silence keeps them out of hearing of predators. A home health check does not take long (it can even be completed during grooming), and can help you determine if there is a problem (see chapter 16).

No. 7

RIDING STYLES AND DISCIPLINES

ENGLISH AND WESTERN

English riding evolved in Europe and was based on military horse regimens. Western riding evolved in the American West, to meet the needs of cowboys. Despite their contrasting origins, there are fewer differences between the two styles than most people think. Central to both are the communication and cooperation between horse and rider, which is important for controlling the horse in a variety of situations. The main differences are in the method of control and the type of equipment (tack) used. Within each style are many disciplines, which vary in description and popularity, based on organization and geography.

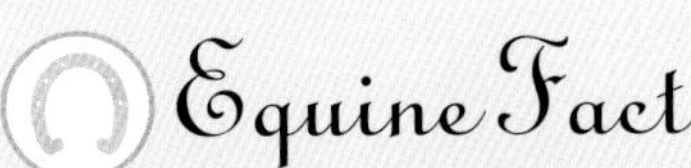

Equine Fact

Regardless of what style a horse is trained for, he can be ridden by an English or Western rider, with just a few adjustments.

English riding has a long tradition in Europe, with enthusiasts worldwide. Given its military background, it's not surprising that it's viewed as the more formal riding style. This is further enhanced because of the tack used and because English riders are typically more formally dressed in competition.

English tack: The English saddle is smaller, lighter, and designed to give the rider closer contact with the horse's back. Reins are held in both hands and used as aids—along with the seat, leg, and sometimes a riding crop—to communicate direction and speed. The bit used is specific to English riding, to maximize rein control via the horse's mouth.

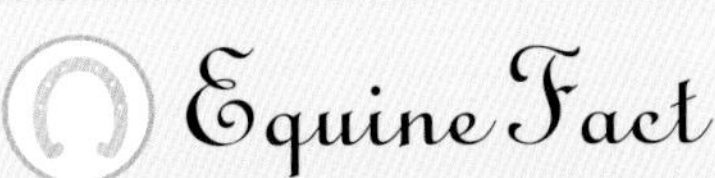

Equine Fact

With both the English and the Western saddle there are different designs available to accommodate certain sports and disciplines.

BEHIND THE SIGNS

Cowboy Style

Western horses are trained to neck rein, meaning they will change direction with only the light pressure of a rein against their neck. This enables control of the horse with one hand, freeing up the other hand for work on the range, such as the use of a lasso, or lariat, to rope cattle or perform other necessary tasks. In contrast, riders trained in English riding style hold a rein in each hand to communicate with their horse.

Western riding comes from the ranching traditions of the American West, with the equipment and riding style evolving to meet the working needs of the cowboy. Today it is recreational for the most part, although Western riding is still used in ranching and farming.

Western tack: The Western saddle is larger and heavier. It's designed to spread the weight of the rider more evenly over the horse's back, maximizing the horse and rider's comfort during long rides over rough terrain. Its working background means that it has a forward horn, used to drape the lasso or roping lariat. There is lighter rein contact in Western riding, with reins held in one hand to leave the second hand free for jobs like roping cattle. The rider uses his weight—along with neck reining and sometimes spurs—to give aids or cues to the horse.

AIDS OR CUES?

You will hear both terms as you do your research into riding styles. When you start lessons you may be told to use your reins as aids, or to cue your horse with the reins. The two terms are often used interchangeably to describe using reins, legs, or weight to communicate with your horse. Some enthusiasts believe that aids refer only to the pressure used to communicate, while cues refer to conditioned responses. Others don't differentiate between the two. After all, the horse doesn't care what term you use, as long as he understands your message.

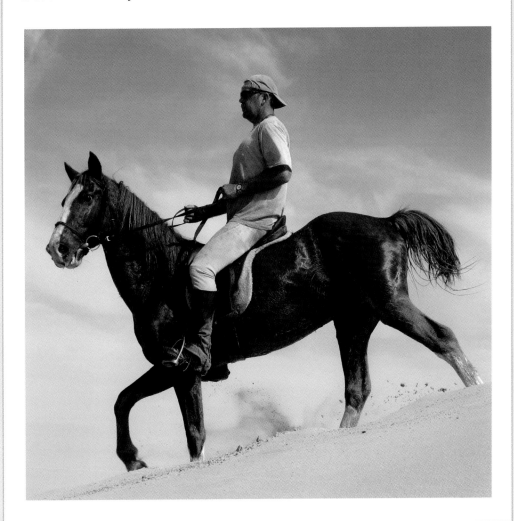

RIDING POSITION

Both styles require riders to have a solid seat. The rider should sit tall, with the hips and shoulders balanced over the feet. Arms should be relaxed and against the rider's side, with legs hanging naturally against the horse's sides. In English riding, a rein is held in each hand, whereas in Western riding one hand holds the reins and the other hand rests on the rider's thigh or side.

DISCIPLINES AND EVENTS

Competing is not necessary to enjoy riding. In fact, some find that the pressure of performing, as well as the expense involved, detracts from the time spent with their horse. If competition is for you, however, it's a great way to further involve yourself in the equestrian community and build skills.

Each riding style has different activities that riders can compete in. Common Western riding sports include barrel racing, roping, trail classes, and Western pleasure. Some of the many English riding competitions include dressage, eventing, hunt seat or hunter classes, hunters or jumpers, and saddle seat. There are also some disciplines, such as long-distance endurance riding, in which both Western and English riding styles compete.

BEHIND THE SIGNS

Then and Now

Hunt seat and jumping evolved from the practice of hunting, while dressage has its origin in military training. Rodeo events began as a way to champion ranching skills. Sidesaddle dates back to the days when female riders rode aside, rather than astride, a horse, and celebrates this equestrian style by continuing to be practiced at competitive levels. Other events, such as harness racing, began with the spontaneous competition between drivers on the roads. Today, these disciplines hold true to their traditions, while continuing to evolve.

DIFFICULTY LEVEL?

Both English and Western riding take training and practice. Most experts agree, though, that even a novice can enjoy an afternoon of Western riding, while English riding may prove more of a challenge at first. This is because the larger saddle used in Western riding provides more stability. Western-trained horses also "jog," a slower gait that makes balance easier for most. English-trained horses use a bouncy gait, which usually requires more of an adjustment.

For practiced English riders, the transition to Western is relatively straightforward, but this is not usually the case when the roles are reversed (Western to English riding).

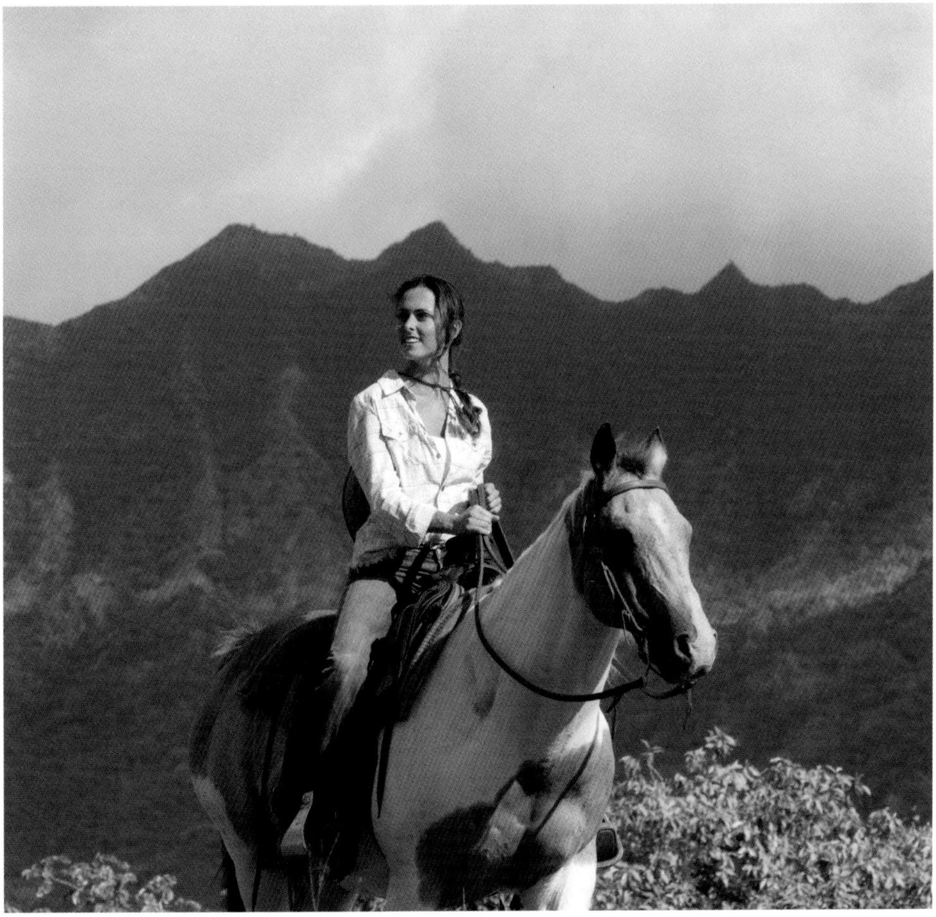

WESTERN RIDING DISCIPLINES

Barrel Racing is a speed sport in which horse and rider negotiate a triangle pattern of preset barrels that are placed in the center of the arena. Precision—turning tightly around each barrel without going too wide—is important as this is a timed event and points are deducted if a barrel is knocked over. At youth and amateur levels, male and female riders compete. At the professional level it's primarily an event for women.

Roping Events are one of the oldest of rodeo sports. They are based on what cowboys and ranchers have traditionally done daily: moving cattle across long distances and pulling them to safety as needed, and gathering animals for branding or medical treatment. In these events—of which there are many—riders compete to lasso and tie the legs of calves and steers, with the winner chosen for best time and maneuvering. Roping events include breakaway roping, calf roping, steer roping, and team roping.

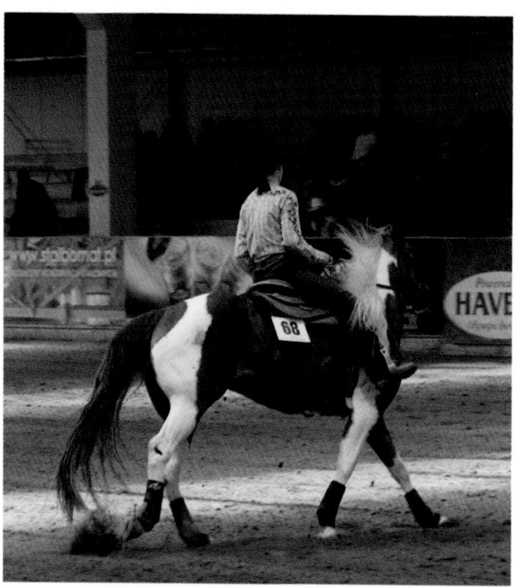

Trail Classes are an arena event in which the horse and rider must navigate obstacles. These may include gates, a bridge, wooden poles, and anything commonly found on a trail. Judging is based on the horse's obedience, responsiveness, and maneuverability.

Western Pleasure is a show class, in which horses are judged for their appearance, movement, and style. To win they must have a smooth and pleasant gait, and a calm temperament with a responsive disposition. Horses are shown as a group in the arena, and so this is a good introduction to the show ring for the novice.

Equine Fact

A Pleasure class is when the horse is judged. An Equitation class is when the rider's skill is judged.

BEHIND THE SIGNS

Which Breed?

For most events, any breed that is physically capable can be entered. At the lower levels you'll see many different breeds, with the Thoroughbred, Thoroughbred cross breeds, and warmbloods most often dominating the top levels of competition.

Some breeds have been bred for a certain purpose. For example, the American Quarter Horse excels at Western events and sprints, while the Thoroughbred has the endurance and speed necessary for long-distance racing events (see chapter 3).

BEHIND THE SIGNS

Lipizzans, the Dancing Horses

Lipizzan horses are trained in the art of dressage from the Spanish Riding School in Vienna. They perform balletlike movements including choreographed "dances" in which they weave in and out, trot in place, and leap into the air.

ENGLISH RIDING DISCIPLINES

Dressage involves horse and rider performing a set pattern of complex maneuvers. To the observer it may look like dancing, with the routines made up of figure eights, pirouettes, and half passes, as well as changes of pace and direction.

Eventing, or combined training, comprises one round each of dressage, showjumping, and cross-country jumping. There are two main formats: one-day eventing (ODE) and three-day eventing (3DE). The latter is the format used at the Olympics, in which each round is held on a different day.

Hunt Seat or **Hunter Classes** involves riding both flat (nonjumping) and over fences (jumping) demonstrations. Judging is based on form and movement. It is a style of forward seat riding, using a specific saddle, and based on the history of fox hunting.

Hunter or Jumper is a show event in which horses are judged on their movement and manners, particularly while jumping fences. It uses the hunt seat-style tack.

Saddle Seat events are designed to show off a horse's animated gait. It is energetic, with lots of high-stepping, or trotting. Horses are typically trained to do five gaits: the walk, trot, and canter, plus the slow gait and the rack (a four-beat gait). The American Saddlebred, Racking Horse, and Tennessee Walking Horse, among others, are often found at these events.

No. 8

LEARNING CURVE

RIDING LESSONS AND TRAINING

Word-of-mouth is often the best way to find an instructor but, when that's not possible, research can help you find a skilled and suitable teacher. Look to breeder groups and your local and national horse society to find listings of qualified instructors. Do they specialize in teaching novice riders, or in a certain style or discipline? There are many instructors, but the one for you must be a match for your training needs.

Think safety—it is a good instructor's primary concern. They will incorporate it into every lesson. And, because accidents happen, they also maintain up-to-date first-aid qualifications and the necessary insurance cover.

Know what questions to ask, what to expect, and what your role in the learning curve is.

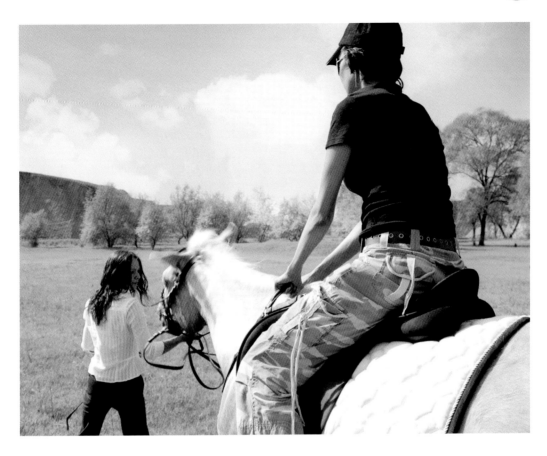

FINDING AN INSTRUCTOR

Once you have done your research and narrowed potential instructors down, you will want to visit the riding facility. Ask to observe a lesson given to someone close to your ability level if possible, or pay for a sample lesson. It will help you decide if you feel comfortable with the instructor and their teaching methods.

Spend some time observing the facility. Is it well kept? Are the horses well looked after? Does the instructor have a good rapport with other staff, and do they seem to enjoy their jobs? Are the people you encounter in the barn and the rest of the facility friendly or is the environment intimidating? Do the people seem to be welcoming or divided into cliques?

Talk to potential instructors about your goals. Are you hoping to get involved in competition? Or are you more interested in building your riding confidence through casual riding? You want an instructor who will be realistic with you, and give you an idea of the game plan based on your aims.

QUESTIONS TO ASK POTENTIAL INSTRUCTORS

WHAT CERTIFICATIONS DO YOU HOLD?
Certifications through several organizations are available, dependent on location.

HOW LONG HAVE YOU BEEN COACHING?
The amount of time doesn't reflect ability, but a passion for horses is not enough. Teaching experience is a definite plus.

DO YOU HAVE A SPECIALTY?
This is especially important if you have decided on a certain discipline or activity. Breed clubs and organizations can provide valuable information, and help point you in the direction of suitable instructors.

CAN YOU PROVIDE STUDENT REFERENCES?
If possible, ask for the references' contact information, so that you can talk to them about the teaching style and any successes they've experienced.

WHAT IS THE STUDENT–TEACHER RATIO IN LESSONS?
Safety is one of the most important considerations. Generally, the smaller the student–teacher ratio, the better the supervision you will receive. Group classes can add extra motivation as well as help you meet others with shared interests. Private classes can translate to personalized instruction at your pace.

HOW MUCH?
Of course, the cost of lessons is a factor, but it should not be your only consideration.

TRAINING

Training will vary according to instructor, but most have in common the following elements:

PRE-LESSON

An instructor may give homework, in the form of a video to watch or reading material. This helps to prepare you by providing a mental picture of what you will be doing in the lesson. Visualization can also provide a sense of security, because you'll know what to expect. There will still be surprises, but preparation can help set you at ease.

THE LESSONS

If you are a novice, the initial lesson will teach you to safely mount and dismount. Once you have mastered this, and there is no rush or time limit, you will then be shown the basic rider position and the posture you should use. Next, you will be shown how to walk your horse forward and how to change direction. These are the introductory basics, all of which will be reviewed over a number of lessons as you continue to progress.

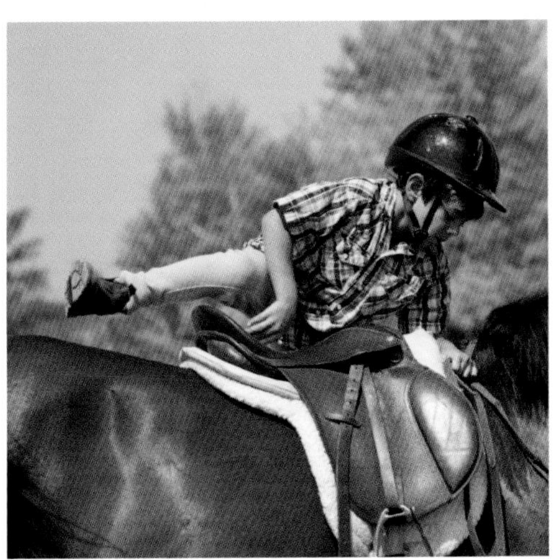

It's not in the riding facility's interest to scare you away from the sport, so any reputable facility will ensure you are comfortable with each step in your training. They will also start you on a docile horse, perfectly suited to a novice rider.

Lessons should start with a warm-up, followed by a review of the previous lesson if applicable. A review is important as it establishes whether you and the horse are ready for the next step. Each new lesson should build on past lessons. The review helps you and the instructor decide whether this lesson will focus on the same elements as the last lesson, perhaps with a different approach, or if you are ready to move to the next step.

BEHIND THE SIGNS

Horse and Equipment

It doesn't make sense to invest in a horse or equipment before you start lessons. In the meantime, the riding facility should be able to loan you everything you need, from horse to helmet. Reputable riding schools will take great care in matching your temperament to that of the horse.

Once you have decided that riding is for you, the next step is determining the type of riding you will be involved in. Riding style will dictate the type of horse and gear necessary.

Most students learn by doing, combined with seeing and hearing. For this reason, experienced instructors will include practical components in which demonstrations are used to show, for example, the correct body position.

YOUR ROLE

What is your goal? Communicate this to your instructor well in advance so that you can discuss its feasibility, and lesson plans can be adjusted if necessary.

Be early for your lesson in order to get the most out of it. You want to be relaxed by the time the lesson starts, so you can fully enjoy and concentrate on the instruction. You will also need time before the lesson to groom the horse—and you don't want to rush this—and tack up, both of which you will be taught in your first few lessons. Take some time to review your last lesson, so you can start this session with any questions. It shouldn't really need to be said but, just in case you haven't thought of it, turn your phone off. Not only could the ringtone spook the horse, you should also be totally focused on where you are and what you're doing, not where you were an hour ago or where you're heading after the lesson has finished.

If you've done your research thoroughly, you will find yourself a reputable riding facility. You're there to learn, so listen to what they have to say. Don't get frustrated. Focus. Comparing yourself to other riders will not help your progress. Instead, concentrate on building your own skills. Practice does eventually make perfect, but there will be inevitable stumbling blocks when learning a new skill.

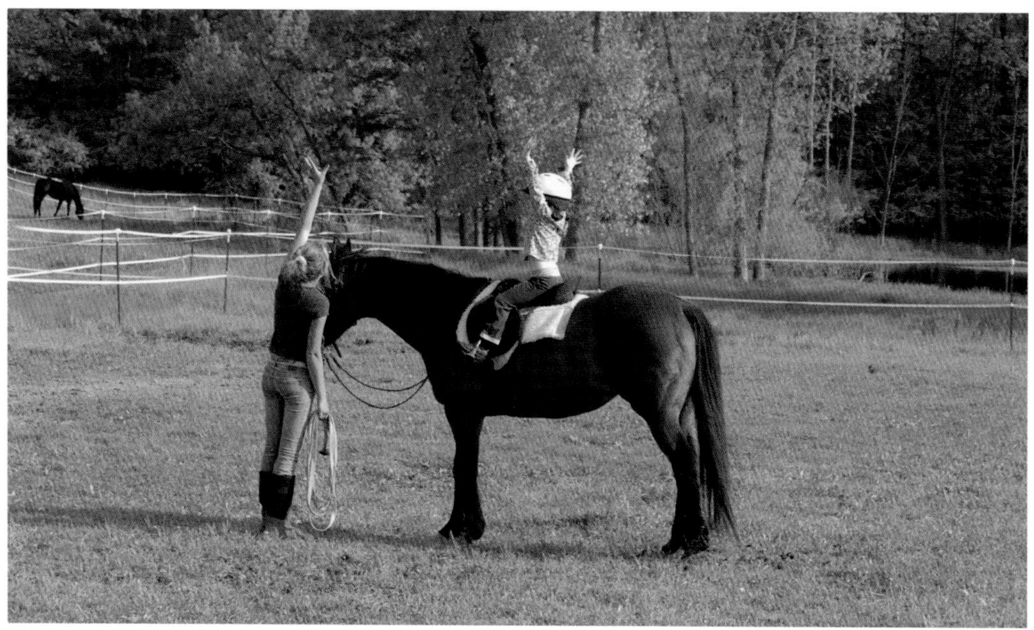

Make notes after each lesson, while it is still fresh in your mind. What were you taught? What did you find especially difficult? What needs further clarification? What mechanical clarifications did your instructor provide? Were you told—perhaps multiple times—to keep your posture straight or your heels down? Remember this and try to apply it in the next lesson. Work on your physical fitness. Balance and coordination, endurance, flexibility, and strength are all necessary to advance as a rider.

Speak to your instructor about the value of unsupervised practice—at the novice stage there are positives and negatives. Practicing balance, stop and go, and more are all good, but repeated incorrect use of aids can frustrate the horse to the point whereby he's no longer cooperative. If he doesn't know what is expected of him, he may simply stop responding, and this can erode any trust you've built and cause you to take a few steps back.

THE INSTRUCTOR'S ROLE

The instructor should involve you in their plan to help you reach your goals. They should outline small goals—finally getting a transition smooth, for example—as well as larger, down-the-road goals, such as your first competition. They should be honest and realistic. Will you need new tack, or even a new horse?

It's the instructor's responsibility to make you feel at ease and to be approachable so that you're comfortable asking questions and expressing any concerns. They should make every effort to maintain your confidence. The instructor should challenge you to progress, while knowing just how far they can realistically push at this point in your training. The instructor is also responsible for the safety and well-being of the horse and student during the lesson. This should be their first concern, with everything else revolving around safety.

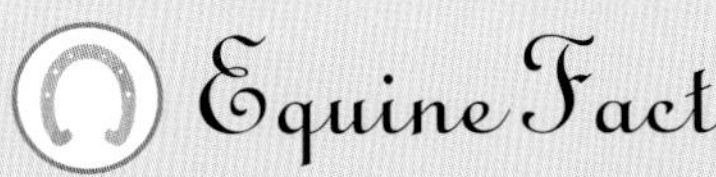

Equine Fact

Not all riding instructors are licensed by law. Some areas mandate they must be, while others don't.

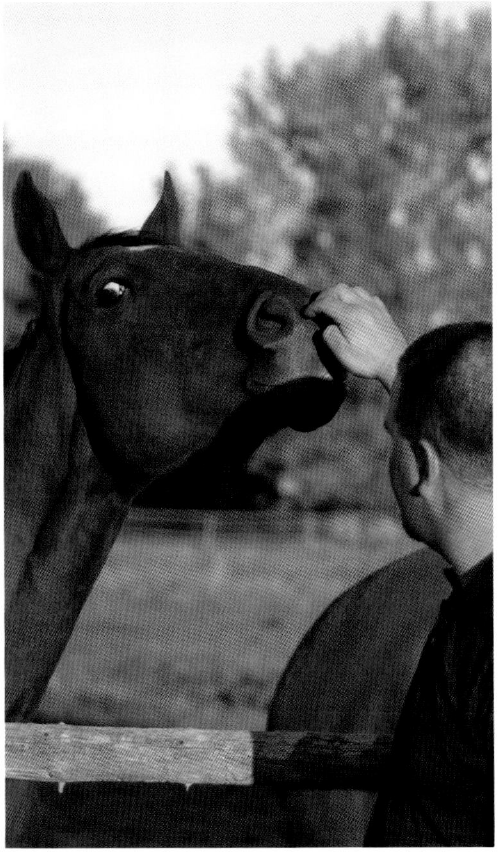

BEHIND THE SIGNS

Move at Your Own Pace

It's not about learning to ride quickly, it's about learning to ride correctly. There are many factors that influence learning to ride a horse. No rider learns or progresses exactly as another does; each individual will vary at each stage of learning. In general, you'll spend your first couple of lessons getting used to how the horse moves. You'll practice balance in the saddle and the correct seat. You'll learn how to stop and how to go, after which you will proceed to the trot, which can be ridden in two ways: rising and sitting.

No. 9

TACKING UP

SADDLING AND BRIDLING KNOW-HOW

"Tacking up" refers to the saddling and bridling of the horse. The bridle is the horse's headgear, which includes the bit and reins. Always saddle first, bridle last. Saddle the horse just before you plan on riding, and when you are ready to bridle the horse. In this way the horse remains safely tied up with the halter throughout saddling. Bridles should not be used to secure a horse. Halters are the correct method.

Saddling and bridling are essentially the same whether you use English or Western tack, but any differences are noted on the left side of the step-by-step instructions below. The directions may look like a lot to wrap your head around, but after a couple of supervised practice sessions it will all flow very quickly. Seeing really is understanding. There is no substitute to watching a horse professional tack up and take you through the process. These directions are a guide, but are not enough to go it alone. Saddling and bridling are too important to get wrong, so one-on-one instruction is necessary.

SADDLING YOUR HORSE

Regardless of the type of saddle you are using, the general process will be as follows:

1. English & Western: Approach the horse softly, and speak to him throughout the process of tacking up. Have everything you need at hand.

2. English & Western: Use the horse's halter (the head harness) to secure your horse to crossties or a hitching post, in a quiet area where there is nothing to distract him. Crossties should be long enough for the horse to lower his head comfortably, but short enough that he can't become entangled in the rope.

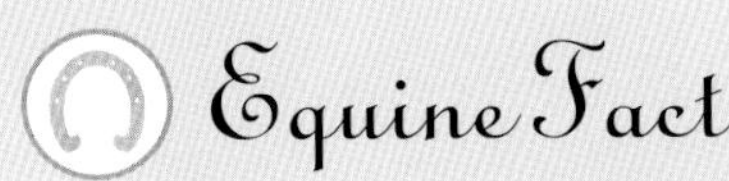

The saddle blanket should extend further than the saddle, to protect the horse and make the saddle more comfortable.

3. English & Western: Groom your horse. This is to make sure the coat is free of any hair clumps, dirt, or bedding that could cause irritation once the saddle (and rider) presses down on the horse's back. (See chapter 15).

4. English & Western: Check that the saddle cloth you are using is clean and dry, with no debris that could cause irritation. Working from the horse's left side, place the top edge of the saddle cloth at his withers. Slide the rest of the cloth down over the saddle area in the direction of the hair, to prevent the hair clumping.

Equine Fact

Keep a hand on the horse's rump as you change sides (unless you move well away from him). This way your horse is aware of what you are doing, and there are no sudden movements that might startle him or cause him to kick.

5. Western Only: Lay the right stirrup and cinch over the saddle's seat or horn, so when you put the saddle on the horse (from the left side) they don't swing down and hit the horse. (The cinch is permanently attached to the right side of Western saddles.)

6. English & Western: Raise the saddle as high and let it down gently on the back of the horse, just below the withers. There should be 2–3 inches (5–8 cm) of the saddle cloth showing in front and behind the saddle. If not, the cloth is too short, and there's a good possibility it may work itself under the saddle.

7a. English Only: Attach the saddle cloth to the saddle by threading the middle girth strap through the loop provided on the cloth. Attach the same two straps from both sides of the horse to the buckles. When moving to the opposite side of the horse either stay very close or well back (to avoid a potential kick).

7b. Western Only: Move to the opposite side, either staying very close to the horse or well back from his heels (in case of a kick). Let the stirrup and cinch down from where you had placed it on the seat or horn. Return to the left side, and reach under the horse to catch the front cinch. Secure this by placing its strap into the buckle. Next, secure the rear cinch if there is one. If there is not a buckle then a Western cinch knot can be used. Leave enough room between the horse's belly and the back cinch for the flat of your hand to fit.

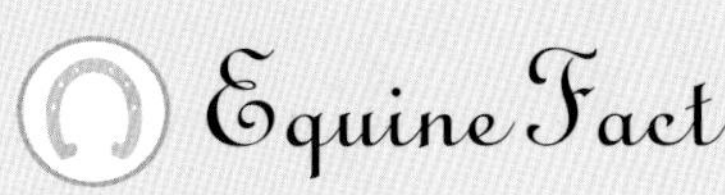

Unsaddling is the reverse of saddling, starting with your final step when tacking up and moving up.

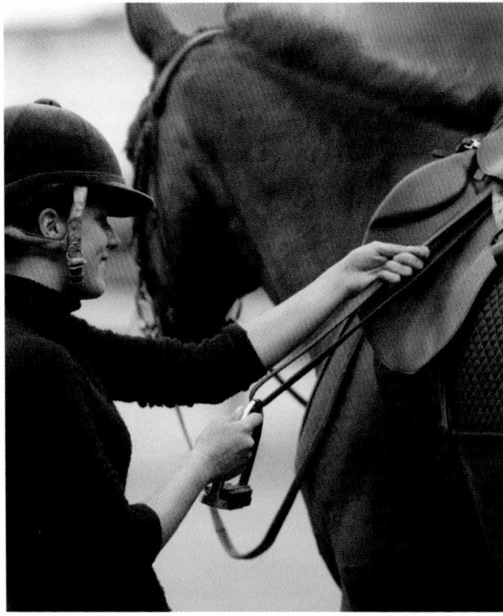

8. English & Western: Once you have put the bridle on (instructions to follow), tighten the girth or cinch further. This method is especially useful when dealing with a horse that puffs out his stomach when the saddle is first put on because it gives his stomach time to return to normal before saddling is complete. When the girth has had its final tightening, stand in front of the horse and pull each foreleg forward. This will ensure that skin has not been caught or wrinkled under the girth or cinch, which could make for a painful ride.

9. English & Western: Adjust the stirrups before mounting. In practice sessions you will have established the correct length for your legs. When mounted, double-check stirrup length, by hanging your legs at the horse's side (your feet should not be in stirrups for this test). If the stirrup irons rest at your ankles this is generally the correct length, although Western riders often wear their stirrups longer.

BRIDLING YOUR HORSE

Once you have groomed and saddled your horse you are ready to bridle him:

1. English & Western: To get the bridle on you will need to move the halter that you put on to secure the horse at the start of saddling. To do this, stand at the horse's head, unbuckle the halter so you can now on fit it around the horse's neck, and rebuckle. At this point the horse is no longer tied up, which is why the bridle should always go on just before you ride.

2. English & Western: Put the reins over the horse's head so they lay across his neck.

3. English & Western: Stand next to the horse's head, facing the same direction (and again, remember you always start from the left side of the horse). Holding the bridle (headpiece) in your right hand, put that arm between the horse's ears. Do this from behind, so that the hand holding the bridle ends up at the front of the horse's head. Most horses

will drop their heads at this, which will make it easier to lift and guide the bridle onto the horse's ears. Hold the bit in your left hand, just in front of the horse's mouth. Carefully insert the bit into his mouth, being extra careful not to bang it against teeth or lips. You may need to encourage the horse to open up first by pressing gently against the inside corner of his mouth with your left thumb.

4. English & Western: Slide the bridle over the horse's ears, smoothing any hair that is caught.

5a. English Only: Tighten the throatlatch and noseband, leaving enough room to fit three fingers between the straps and the horse's face.

5b. Western Only: Complete the above step if needed (dependent on the type of Western bridle being used).

6. English & Western: Consider the tacking complete! At this point you are ready to ride.

BEHIND THE SIGNS

Watch and Learn

Incorrect saddling and bridling can result in discomfort or injury—it can lead to the horse experiencing back pain and an incorrect posture and gait. Have an experienced rider or horse professional demonstrate the process multiple times, and work under their supervision for your first two or three tacking-up attempts. Proper saddling is instrumental to the care, comfort, health, and longevity of your horse.

BEHIND THE SIGNS

Unsaddle upon Return

Don't leave a horse standing around with his saddle on when you finish riding. Your horse may decide he'd like to roll, to stretch out after being ridden. If so, he won't be thinking of the saddle still on his back. This could damage the saddle and—more importantly—it could harm your horse, so it is the first thing that should be done upon your return to the stable. It only takes a few minutes to unsaddle your horse and therefore avoid a preventable accident happening. Safety first is always the best policy.

USEFUL TERMS

Bit: Part of the bridle. The piece that goes into the mouth of the horse, and to which the headpiece and the reins are attached. Used to communicate with the horse.

Bridle: Headgear used to direct a horse.

Cinch / Girth: Known as the former in Western riding, and the latter in English riding. It is the wide strap (or straps) that goes under the horse, to secure the saddle.

Crossties: Used to secure your horse, while grooming or tacking up.

Headpiece: The part of the bridle that goes over the horse's ears. It is attached to the bit.

Horn: Located on the front part of the Western saddle, used to hold the lasso (or lariat) for roping cattle.

Latigo (or cinch tiestrap): The strap that connects the cinch to the saddle's rigging.

Reins: The leather straps held by the rider that connect to the bit.

WESTERN CINCH KNOT (ALSO KNOWN AS THE COWBOY KNOT)

Western saddles use a cinch and a cinch strap (or latigo) to secure the saddle to the horse. The cinch strap is attached to the cinch by either buckles or a Western cinch knot.

Today most saddles will use buckles, which makes it easier for novices who may not know the knot, and already have their heads full with the tacking up process.

No. 10

CONTROL AND SAFETY

CLEAR COMMUNICATION FROM THE SADDLE

It's never too late to become a proficient rider. Every rider starts at the beginning: your instructor, the advanced riders at the stable—they all started as novices.

To develop clear communication with your horse, lessons are imperative. They will teach you how to bring the following guide to life, and correctly communicate with your horse when you mount, dismount, position yourself in the saddle, hold the reins, and cue your horse.

HOW TO GET ON YOUR HORSE

As a novice you may feel your horse is too big for you, making mounting impossible. But that's not the case. Once you develop a mounting technique you'll find that, with practice, getting on your horse gets easier and easier.

Mounting is a challenge for many riders, even experienced riders. A mounting block can help, particularly if your riding style is English (and therefore your stirrups are shorter than Western riders'). It makes mounting easier, because it provides height so that you can swing your leg over the horse with less difficulty than if you were on the ground. It's also better for your horse's back and easier on your saddle—reducing strain in both instances. Unfortunately, although there is nothing wrong with using a mounting block, one won't always be available. You will need to learn how to mount from the ground as well. To start:

1. Do a final check of tack. For example, is the girth or cinch snug? This will help prevent the saddle from moving as you mount. If you are riding English you may want to lengthen the stirrups to assist with mounting, and adjust once you are on the horse.

2. Lead your horse to the area where you plan to ride. Have a spotter available to hold the horse's bridle while you practice mounting.

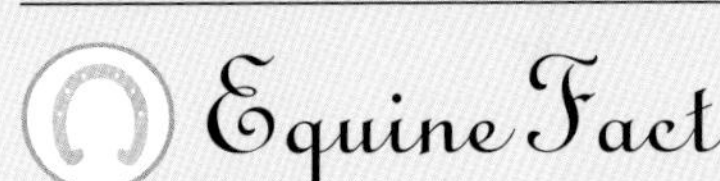

If your horse is tall you may want to drop the stirrup a few holes so that you can reach it, or you may choose to use a stirrup extender. Don't forget to readjust the stirrup length once mounted.

During this maneuver, the majority of your momentum must come from pushing down with your left leg into the stirrup. The back of the saddle will provide leverage as you swing your body upward. Your legs should be doing most of the work here, not your arms.

6. Swing your leg over the horse's hindquarters, being careful to lift your leg high so you do not hit the horse with it.

7. Seat yourself, arrange the reins for riding, put your right foot in the stirrup, and adjust your stirrup length if necessary. You are ready to go!

Of course, it's easier said than done. But, as with any time spent with horses, it can be a lot of fun practicing. You will get it eventually!

3. Stand on the horse's left side, facing the back of the horse. If you are riding English, hold both reins in your left hand, leaving them slack on the right side. Also with your left hand, grasp some of the horse's mane from the base of his neck. Or, if you are riding Western, hold both reins in your left hand, leaving some slack on the right side. Also with your left hand, grasp the saddle horn.

4. Use your right hand to move the stirrup toward you, and put your left foot in it.

5. Grab the back of the saddle (the cantle) with your right hand. Bounce on your right foot a few times, to help propel yourself up. Push off, putting your weight onto your left foot that is in the stirrup. The closer to the horse you stand, the more successful you will be.

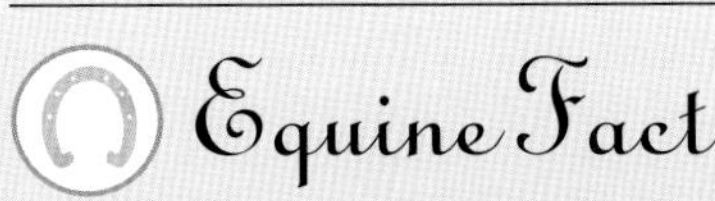

Equine Fact

Never try and mount or dismount while moving. It will confuse your horse, and it is dangerous. Instead, bring your horse to a stop and try again.

HOW TO GET OFF YOUR HORSE

Although much easier than mounting, it may still take some practice to correctly dismount. To start:

1. Bring your horse to a stop. You may want to have someone hold onto the horse's bridle to keep him still while you dismount, especially in the early stages.

2. Grasp both reins in your left hand, leaving them slack on the right side. If necessary, use them to pull the horse up as he moves forward.

3. Stand up in the stirrups, and swing your right leg over the horse's hindquarters.

4. Put your right hand on the back of the saddle (resting your weight on it), free your left foot from the stirrup, and push off. Don't push the horse away as you do so; simply release.

5. Bend your knee as you land, to absorb the shock of landing.

6. Grasp the reins close to the bit with your right hand, lifting the reins over the horse's head to lead it away.

BEHIND THE SIGNS

Core Skills

A correct seat in the saddle is the first step to achieving any success as a rider, regardless of your riding style or activity. It provides you with balance in the saddle, and it helps the horse perform to his best ability by equally distributing your weight across his back. As you practice the correct rider position and learn to ride from your core, you will eliminate bouncing, and will flow with the horse by allowing him to move you with his rhythm.

CUES, IN BRIEF

To communicate with your horse you will use your leg, hand, seat, and/or voice.

For example, in English riding, to turn right you would:

1. Pull back, applying a slight pressure on the rein in your right hand. The left rein should continue to be held in a relaxed manner (neither too tight nor too slack).

2. At the same time, apply pressure with your right leg to the horse's side, to additionally cue the horse.

3. As the horse obeys the cue, stop the pressure from hand and leg. Between cues hold the reins gently, in a happy compromise between slack and tight, keeping contact with the bit until the next cue is given.

In Western riding, to turn right you would:

1. Hold both reins in your left hand, lift your hand slightly, and move it to the right. The left rein should cross the back of the horse's neck as it moves to the opposite side. This is known as neck-reining. No pressure is needed on the bit.

2. At the same time, apply pressure with your right leg to the horse's side, to additionally cue the horse.

3. As the horse obeys the cue, stop the pressure from hand and leg. Bring the reins back to center.

CORRECT SADDLE POSITION

Correct rider position will help you to be more comfortable in the saddle, and it will help your horse to bear your weight safely. Sit in the middle of the saddle, at the lowest part. Your legs should be slightly bent, with the balls of your feet resting on the stirrup bars. Toes should point forward, with the heels pointing down.

If you are in the correct position, an imaginary straight line should be possible from your heels to hips to shoulders and head.

HOW TO HOLD THE REINS

English riding: Hold the reins just above the withers, with a hand for each rein. To move your hands into the correct position, grasp the reins, with your fingers curled and facing down. Place your little fingers and thumb under each rein (all other fingers remain in the grasping position). Turn your hand, so your knuckles face forward and your thumb is on top.

Western riding: Hold the reins just above the withers, in your left hand only. Then, depending on your instructor, you may be asked to practice one of two positions used to hold the reins: 1) Traditional—make a fist with all but the thumb knuckles facing forward. Rest the rein between your thumb and your forefinger. 2) California—make a fist with your left hand and grasp the reins. With your right hand, hold the excess from the reins, while resting that hand on your thigh.

As you practice rein position, be careful not to balance yourself with the reins. It will soon feel very natural!

No. 11

CHOOSING A HORSE

CRITERIA AND CONFORMATION

Buying a horse is a big and often expensive decision. The return is great, but so is the investment in time and money. There's no such thing as the perfect horse, but there is the horse that's perfect for you. Research is needed to find your best equine match—one that has a good temperament, rides well, is healthy, and is suitable for the type and amount of riding you have planned.

Establishing criteria will help in the decision-making process, as can understanding horse conformation. Criteria will involve factors such as the horse's price and age. Conformation will look at the horse's physical characteristics, to see if he is fit for the activity you're most interested in. He may be a wonderful horse for hacking, for example, but not for barrel racing. Criteria will help you narrow down your options, with conformation helping you to establish suitability.

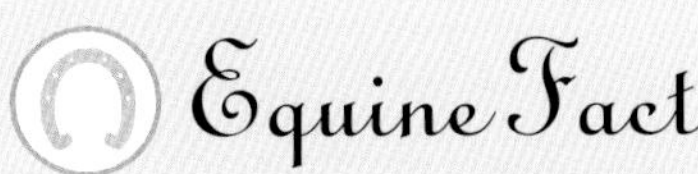

In terms of horse ownership the purchase price of your horse is typically one of the smaller costs. The investment in time and money necessary to care for your horse throughout his life are much greater.

CRITERIA

Establishing a wish list is the first step. What is important to you and what are your goals?

Age: A younger horse may be more suited for a rider with experience, as these horses are typically more mischievous and may be easily spooked. An older horse of around seven or so is generally more mature, calm, and less easily frightened. With care, horses are generally rideable into their twenties.

Breed: Is breed important to you? If so, have you researched breeds through horse owners and breed associations? The breed or type of horse you select should depend on the style of riding you plan to pursue. For example, if you are interested in pleasure riding, there will be horses of almost any breed that will be suitable.

Gender: Mares are generally considered easy-going, although some may be temperamental when in heat. Geldings are also a good mount, although some believe these males to be more prone to stubbornness. It really varies by horse; stallions are typically dominant, and are not easily controlled by the novice or intermediate rider.

Price: How much you are willing to spend will influence the type of riding you do. There are many wonderful horses available that are perfect for the weekend, noncompetitive rider. They tend to be less expensive, with price increasing according to breed and the horse's individual merits. If you are looking to compete at advanced levels, for example, you may be looking for a thoroughbred or warmblood, and the price will generally be on the higher end of the scale.

Size: Who will be riding the horse? They should be able to groom, tack up, mount, and handle the horse on their own.

Temperament: Novice riders should be matched with a horse of calm and easy-going personality, rather than a spirited or stubborn mount. Look for a

Equine Fact

Conformation can tell you if the horse has the physical ability to perform specific tasks.

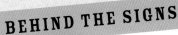

nonaggressive horse and one without stable vices, such as weaving or crib biting, which can be difficult to cure (see chapter 18).

Training: Novice or intermediate riders will need a mount that has been trained. Questions to ask include: What level of training has the horse received? What successes has he had? Is the horse easily ridden and handled by children and adults? Some horses have a marked preference for a certain rider.

CONFORMATION

Equine conformation refers to the whole horse and how everything, from the horse's bone structure, musculature, and body proportions, ties together. It's a method for judging a horse's physical appearance against what the ideal is, for either athletic or breed purposes. Why is this important? If you know what you plan to do with your horse—pleasure riding or the show ring, for example—an understanding of horse conformation can help you pick a horse that is best suited to that activity.

The study of horse conformation is extensive. Below are some of the basics, along with tips on what to look for.

BEHIND THE SIGNS

Soundness and Health

Conformation may be more of a concern the more competitive and advanced your riding style is. However, any horse you consider buying should be in good general health and not suffer from repeat health problems, such as colic. Health problems inhibit performance, are costly, increase the time necessary for daily care, and it can be heartbreaking as an owner to see your horse ill or suffering. Of course, even healthy horses can get sick, but most would agree it's best to start out as you mean to continue, and to do your best through regular grooming and care to keep your horse in good health.

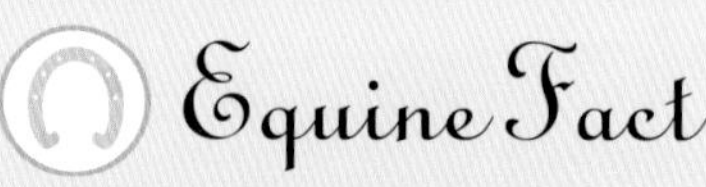

Thoroughbreds typically have large noses and nostrils. This provides better aerobic capacity, and helps them excel at physically challenging events.

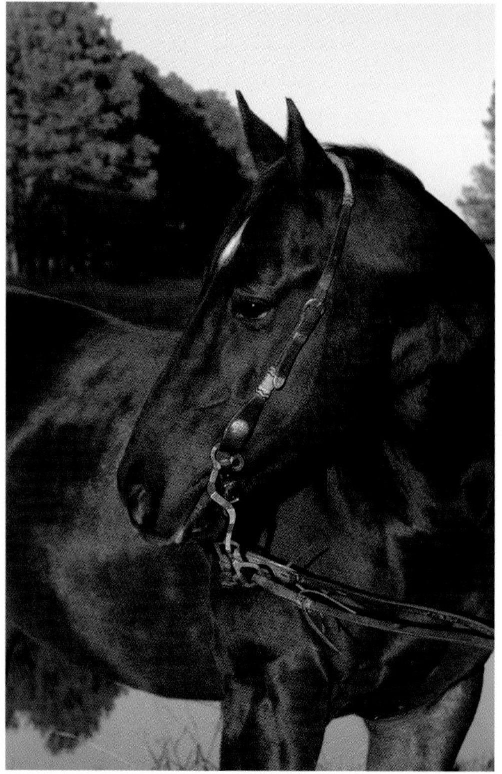

HEAD AND NECK

The head should be in proportion to the rest of the body and should be consistent with breed characteristics. When viewed from the side it should look triangular in appearance, with strong jaws tapering to the muzzle. Since horses aren't able to breathe through their mouth, a large nose and nostrils are considered a good sign, indicating that the horse has good aerobic capacity and will be able to work hard. The eyes and ears provide clues as to the horse's temperament—eyes should be positioned on the sides of the head and should have no white showing (except in the Appaloosa breed, in which the whites of the eye show naturally). Ears should be pricked and alert (not flattened and facing back) to show tractability. A short, thick neck may be a sign of strength, whereas a thin and long neck generally translates to balance and elegance.

CHEST AND BACK

The horse's chest should be wide enough to provide the space needed for his lungs to expand comfortably. If the chest is too narrow he may not be a good choice for athletic activities, as his aerobic capacity is reduced.

The back is very important. The withers (the highest point of a horse's back, where his neck meets the shoulders) should be capable of holding a saddle. If the back is too flat or dips too much (sway-backed) or curves upward (roached back), then fitting the saddle can be problematic.

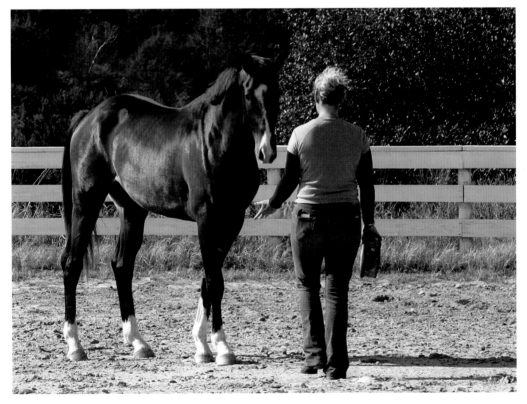

HINDQUARTERS, LEGS, AND FEET

The hindquarters act as the horse's engine, providing the force that moves the horse forward or upward. A hindquarter that is at least 30 percent of the overall horse in length is generally preferable for advanced competition, while 33 percent is considered ideal. Thoroughbreds may exceed this, with some having a hindquarter length reaching 35 percent. Power also comes from the legs, with well-muscled front legs a good indicator of speed.

The front legs carry 60–65 percent of the horse's weight. Therefore, a front leg that has a slight bend toward the hind legs can be a worry, as it may put the tendons under greater strain when jumping, while too much forward bend can also indicate a horse who may have trouble over fences. A horse that is bow-legged (with knees that bend outward) or knock-kneed (with knees that bend inward) may have a problematic gait, and his ability in certain activities may be compromised. The hocks (ankles) must also be correctly angled, otherwise tendon strain can result.

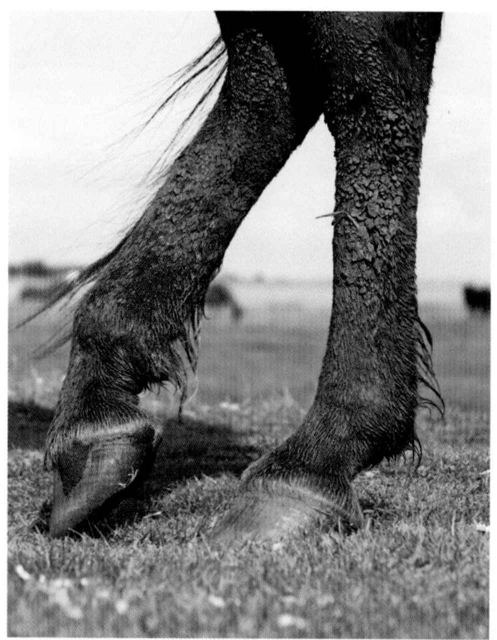

The hooves should be free from cracks and rings. They should stand squarely and evenly on the ground, with toes pointing straight ahead. If the horse is splay-footed (with toes not pointing correctly) he may not move straight.

LOVE AT FIRST SIGHT

It's easy to fall in love with a horse on first meeting, but that does not always translate into a good long-term relationship. See many horses before you decide. Visit stables, breed clubs, horse shows, and training clinics. Talk to trainers, instructors, veterinarians, and horse owners. Hire a well-respected horse professional to go horse shopping with you. It's worth it, as they will have questions you may not know to ask, based on their experience. If possible, this person should be the instructor who has been giving you lessons, and will continue giving you lessons on your new horse. They know your skillset and have a relationship with you. They can also prevent you making a decision based purely on the big brown eyes of a horse, instead of all the factors that will add up to your best equine match.

TO BUY OR NOT TO BUY

As with anything you buy, the seller's reputation is important. Get referrals and do your research. Once you have narrowed down potential horses on paper, you're ready to visit the stables to see them in person. The process involved will typically follow this pattern of evaluation and vetting:

- Watch the horse in his stall to observe his behavior. Does he seem friendly or aggressive?
- Pay attention while the horse is groomed. Is he comfortable being handled? Does he accept the saddle and bridle easily?
- Watch the horse move. Observe the horse at a walk and trot to judge soundness, helped by the expert you have employed to help you make a decision.
- Observe the horse being ridden by his handler to evaluate his training and tractability. Ask what was involved in his training, and any preference the horse shows for riders. Does the horse have any problem behaviors?
- The horse professional you have hired should next ride the horse. They know what you are looking for and will be able to assess whether the horse is a good match.
- You should have a test ride. Is the horse easy to mount? How comfortable is his gait? How responsive is he to your cues? Remember, this is a big purchase and a long-term responsibility.
- Request time to groom the horse so you can see how he reacts to things like having his hooves lifted.
- Ask to see the horse being loaded into his trailer. He should be willing to load, as this will be necessary when transporting him at any time in the future.
- If you decide the horse is a good match, then a pre-purchase veterinary exam is the next step, with a veterinarian of your choice. Some portions of this exam will be covered in the purchase price, while others will be additional—but worthwhile—costs.

BEHIND THE SIGNS

Try, Test, Evaluate

The only way to decide on whether a horse is right for you is to try the horse, have a trusted expert test the horse, and have a veterinarian evaluate the horse's health and soundness.

The horse's ability should be suited to your activity, whether it be hacking or dressage. Their temperament should be a match for the rider's age and experience. For example, a young and excitable horse is not the best match for a young and excitable rider, despite the temptation parents may have to purchase a horse that will grow with their child.

The veterinarian will observe the horse thoroughly and provide a health examination. Their role is not to make a decision for you but to tell you, based on your goals, if the horse has a health problem or is otherwise unfit for your purposes.

- If the horse meets your criteria then you are almost ready to bring him home. The last step is drafting the trial period, lease, or purchase agreement, stating all terms.

TRY BEFORE YOU BUY

Most sellers will agree to a trial period, from a couple of weeks to 30 days. This allows you to get to know the horse and decide if you are suited. Depending on the seller, this may be a lease agreement, with an option to buy. Ensure that all of the terms of the trial or lease are in writing. Many sellers will have insurance that covers the horse during this period; if not, you will need to provide this. You will be responsible for the horse's food, shelter, and care, while the seller is typically responsible for any medical costs during this time.

TRANSLATING "FOR-SALE" ADVERTISEMENTS

The terminology used in horse for-sale advertisements may seem like a different language. It may also vary, according to where you live. Below are some of the abbreviations used (in capitals), along with common terms and their translations.

Auto: Performs movement easily
BA: Breeders Association
BD: British dressage
BE: British eventing
BM: Broodmare
BR: Barrel racer
Easy to do: Is well mannered
END: Endurance horse
Foward going: Responsive to leg aids
GLDNG: Gelding (castrated)
GNTL: Horse with a gentle temperament
Green: Inexperienced horse
HH: Hands high, measurement used to describe the horse's height
HT: Hunter trials
HUS: Hunter under saddle
JMP: Jumps
LDR: Long-distance Riding
LL: Horse has been worked with lunge, or longe line
Loads: Boards trailers easily
LS: For lease
M&F: Mare and foal available
NR: Not registered
ODE: One-day event
OTT: Off the track thoroughbred
PB: Part bred
QH: Quarter horse
REG: Registered with the breeding association
RESC: Rescue horse
RIDES: Has been worked under saddle
SH: Show hunter
SJ: Showjumper
Snaffle mouth or Snaffle ride: Has a responsive mouth; is ridden in a snaffle bit
Sound: No lameness issues
Stud: Stallion (not castrated)
TB: Thoroughbred
Ties: Ties to fences or crossties without fuss
TR: Trail rides
US: Under saddle; with a rider
WB: Warmblood
XC: Cross-country

No. 12

HOUSING YOUR HORSE

OPTIONS AND REQUIREMENTS

Stables do not provide a natural environment for equines. Despite this, they will gladly make the stall their home provided that their needs are met. Happily stabled horses are those that receive daily companionship, exercise, grazing time, care, and grooming.

Done right, a stable can provide a wonderful home for your horse. Whether you choose a stable block or barn, the positioning and design require careful planning. When in doubt as to styles and materials, one simple question will help you decide: What will keep my horse healthy and happy? Think safety and well-being first.

STABLE BLOCK OR BARN

The stable may be a standalone series of stalls, known as a stable block. Or it may be located in a barn with the stable, or stalls, running down each side.

"Location, location, location," so the real estate saying goes. It applies to your barn—the more weather-friendly option—or stable block as well, given this will be your horse's home. A standalone stable block will have less protection from the elements than a barn, so it should be located out of the wind. Both stable block and barn should be situated on well-draining land; it should have a power and water source; vehicle access; and it should be constructed on level ground. Feed storage areas should be kept away from the stables to cut down on fire risk. The muckheap should also be located far enough away to prevent flies and odor.

The larger the stall the better. Horses are not meant to be confined, so the more room they have to move around when stabled the happier they will be. The stall should be at least one and a half times the horse's length, and the height should allow for plenty of headroom. At a minimum, the stable should be 12 ft (3.6 m) square and 9 ft (2.7 m) high.

The stable design should ensure all fittings, from lights and switches to wires, are well out of the horse's reach. Doors should slide or open outward, not inward. The latter is inconvenient and unsafe—it would be very difficult to close or open the door when the horse is in residence. A horseproof bolt on the door is necessary; a kick bolt on the bottom for ease of use and extra security is practical. It provides extra reinforcement in case the horse kicks, and it makes it easy for you to open the stall door with your foot—perfect for when you are leading your horse in or are carrying feed or tools. The bottom half of the door should be at a height that easily allows your horse to see out (generally 4 ft, or 1.2 m, high), perhaps covered with metal to prevent chewing. Natural light is important, so windows, barred on the inside to protect the horse from the glass, and skylights should be part of the design. The former also provides ventilation, so important in stables and necessary to prevent respiratory problems, among other health concerns. An air vent near the roof will also help air flow. Drainage

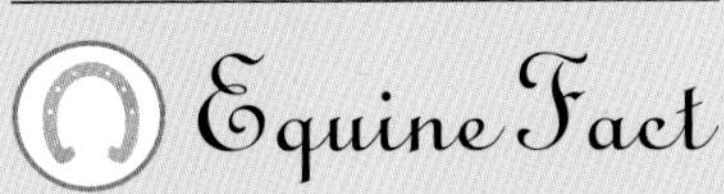

For horses kept at grass year-round it may be necessary to restrict grass in the spring and provide additional feed in the winter.

is another important sanitary consideration; it will also save you money on bedding. Floors should slope slightly to encourage drainage, and should be hardwearing and moisture-resistant. They should be easy to clean thoroughly and have a nonslip surface. Rubber—mats or in brick form—laid over a cement floor is a popular option. It provides a softer surface and is easy to clean. The roof should have efficient guttering and be pitched for drainage. It should have an overhang, to prevent rain blowing in through an open door. The material used for the roof should not create too much noise when hit by rain, or too much heat in summer months.

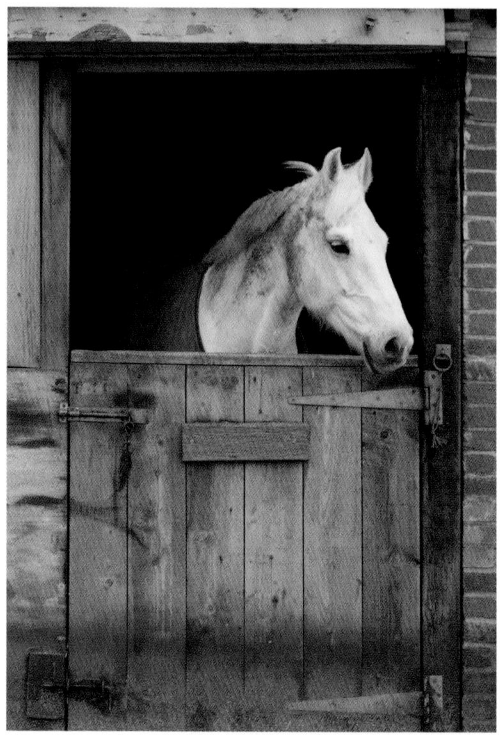

HEALTH AND SAFETY

- The yard area should be fenced.
- Wooden stables and barns will need to be treated annually with fire retardant, as will roofing felt if used.
- Multiple fire extinguishers in easy-to-reach locations (for you, not the horse) should be located throughout the barn or stable block.
- Stables should be airy with good cross-air ventilation—a must to protect your horse's health.
- Feed storage and muckheap should be located at a distance from the stable.
- Surfaces in stables, passageways, and walks should be easy to clean and free of any obstructions that could be a danger.
- Stabled horses are easily bored if isolated, which can lead to stable vices and an unhappy horse. Make sure your horse is able to see out from his stall, at other horses or whatever might be going on around him.

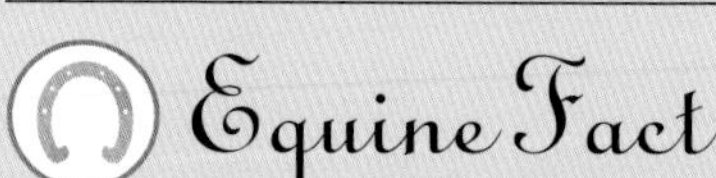

Poorly designed stables can be a health risk and may encourage stable vices, which are a serious concern and can be very difficult to eliminate once developed. (See chapter 18).

OUTDOOR LIVING

Horses are sometimes kept at grass year-round. In this scenario, safety and well-being are again the main considerations. Fields should be fenced and there should be a shelter to protect the horse from the elements. Take your climate into consideration: Will your horse need additional warmth in the winter months? Is there shade for hot summer days? Recommended ratio of pasture to horse varies geographically, but is generally 1.5 acres, or 6,000 square meters.

BEHIND THE SIGNS

Not a Natural Environment

The stable is not a natural environment for horses, but they can be perfectly happy stabled as long as they are provided with plenty of time to behave as nature intended. That means plenty of time for daily grazing, in addition to their exercise requirements. Horses in the wild spend their time grazing. Stabled horses need time in pasture each day to do the same, in addition to their exercise requirements. Wild horses lives as a herd. Domestic horses need the company of their "herd," including other hoofed animals and their owner.

No. 13

EQUINE EQUIPMENT

GETTING INTO GEAR

Tack is the term used to describe the equipment necessary to ride and care for your horse. The type of tack you have will depend on the style of riding and activity you pursue. English and Western tack is specific to each style, and within each riding style are multiple disciplines with unique needs.

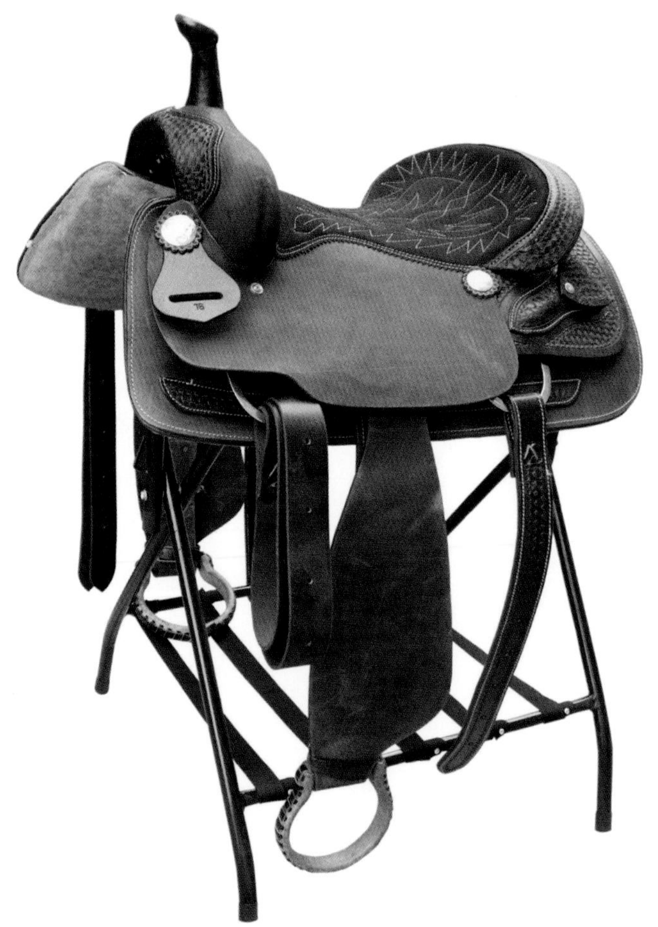

When you first buy tack it will inevitably be expensive, but with care it should last for years. There is so much to choose from it can be overwhelming. Your best bet at the beginning is to stick to the basics and the tried and true. Speak to other horse owners, your riding instructor, staff at the boarding stable, and your veterinarian for recommendations.

THE SADDLE

A saddle is a substantial investment, and one that directly impacts the experience for both the rider and the horse, so it's important to choose wisely. There are different types of saddles for different purposes, such as dressage (English) or roping (Western), as well as general-purpose saddles for nonspecialist riders. Saddles must be fitted correctly, with expert help.

The saddle is made up of components, of which the cantle, skirt, and more contribute, but the stars are the saddle tree, the seat, and the rigging. If these are not correctly designed and constructed, the saddle will not be right, and you and your horse will be at a disadvantage.

Saddle tree: This is the foundation of the saddle. Its job is to distribute the rider's weight over the horse's back, making it more efficient and comfortable for the horse.

Saddle seat: This controls where on the horse's back you will sit, and how comfortable you will be.

Saddle rigging: This is the hardware, the rings and plates, that connect the straps that hold the saddle in place.

Other saddle components include:

Cantle: The back of the saddle that curves upward from behind the seat.

Pommel, or swell: The front end of the saddle.

Skirt: The part of the saddle that lies directly below the rider's upper thighs, protecting their legs from the stirrup bar and auxiliary tack.

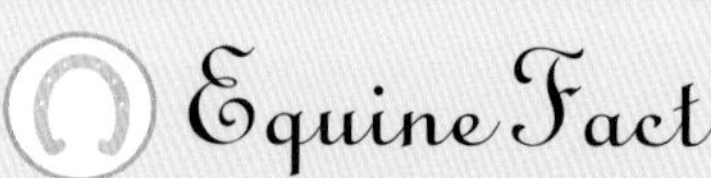

Equine Fact

The English saddle is generally a close-contact saddle, meant to encourage horse and rider communication.

TYPES OF ENGLISH SADDLE

Dressage: A thin and lightweight saddle, to encourage close contact with the horse's back for enhanced communication. The seat is deep for balance, and well padded for comfort.

Jumping (also known as a forward seat or hunt seat): The seat is relatively flat, to facilitate mobility in the saddle. The pommel and cantle are low for an unobstructed position when jumping.

Polo: A flat seat for ease of movement, and unpadded to prevent any obstructions that might slow the rider's response time down.

Racing: The seat is forward and flat. The saddle is very small and very light, to reduce the horse's load and any drag that might slow him down.

Show: Designed to show off a horse's conformation, these saddles are very simple and close-fitting with a flat seat.

Sidesaddle: The seat is comparatively flat and wide to facilitate a rider sitting with both legs on one side of the horse. There are two pommels: the standard pommel and a safety pommel that provides additional stability.

TYPES OF WESTERN SADDLE

Barrel: Designed for speed and stability, the seat is usually deep to keep the rider securely in the saddle while racing, with a high horn for the rider to hold on to during turns.

Cutting: Designed to facilitate "cutting," the process of separating cattle from the larger herd. The seat is flat and long to allow for maximum maneuverability, and it lies close to the horse's back. The swell is high and wide to help keep the rider in the saddle during sharp turns, and the horn is high for increased stability.

Endurance: These saddles differ from other Western saddles because they do not have a horn (to prevent the rider from getting poked in the stomach while jumping trail obstacles, standing while trotting, or posting). Bulk is minimized for a lighter saddle, allowing closer contact with the horse. The seat is heavily padded for comfort, as there are typically long hours in the saddle.

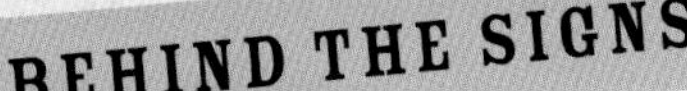

Taking Care of Tack

Given the expense involved in purchasing tack, it makes sense to keep it in good condition. It's also better for your horse. If it doesn't fit properly, it will be uncomfortable for your horse, and he won't perform to the best of his ability. Tack that is dirty can cause skin problems.

Wipe tack down after every ride, and give it a thorough cleaning at least weekly. This may involve using a saddle soap and conditioner to protect the leather of the bridle and saddle. The bit will also need cleaning. Soak it in hot water and use a mild soap, followed by rinsing and polishing.

Pleasure / Trail: Comfort is the priority with these saddles. They are not intended for heavy jobs but are meant for trail riding. They are usually light in weight and often come with a padded seat and a thin horn, but you can choose from a wide variety of trees, horns, swells, seats, and skirt styles.

Reining: The horn and pommel are lower so that they don't interfere with the rider's hands or reins. The saddle is close contact, for increased communication with the horse and a flat seat for sliding stops.

Roping: A deep-seated saddle, designed for demanding use and increased mobility. The horn is tall and strong, as it must be able to withstand the pressure of a roped steer.

Show: The saddle was once the status symbol of the cowboy, and these saddles reflect that. They are highly decorative, with carvings and silver fittings. They are designed more for aesthetics than work, and fashions change frequently. The horn is low so it doesn't obstruct the reins, and the seat has a balance point in its center.

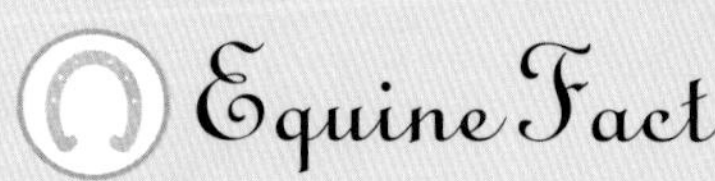

The Western saddle was designed to meet the needs of the working cowboy.

SADDLE FIT

Does the saddle fit you? It should feel comfortable when you sit in it. The correct size of saddle seat is dependent on the rider's size, with larger people needing larger saddles. Children's saddles are usually 13 inches (33 cm) or less, with adult saddle seats 14–18 inches (35–45 cm).

Does the saddle fit your horse? It should sit level on your horse's back and fit securely (without padding). Because of the difficulty in judging fit, and its importance, it's best to get an expert opinion.

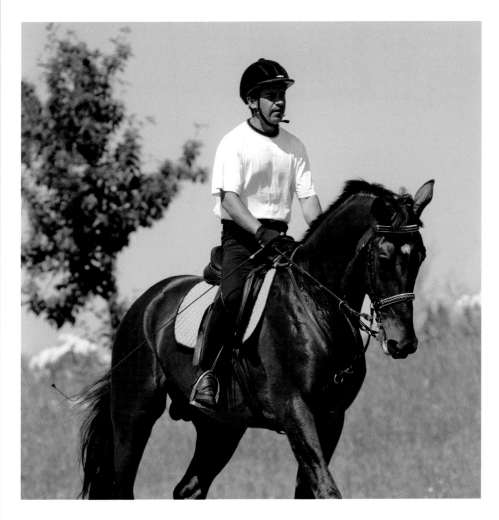

BEHIND THE SIGNS

Form and Function First

Focus less on the name the manufacturer gave the saddle, such as "cutting," "reining," or "roping," and more on how the form of the saddle meets function. Saddlemakers may be superbly talented craftspeople, but they are not necessarily riders. Experienced equestrians can help you make your saddle choice based on your activity, and how well the saddle meets those particular needs. For example, the practicalities of barrel racing necessitate a saddle with a deep seat to keep the rider stable while racing around turns. However, if you take part in jumping events, you'll want a saddle with a flatter seat that allows you to move around easily.

BRIDLE

The bridle is the headgear used to direct a horse. Design varies between Western and English styles, but the main parts of the bridle are the same for both: the headpiece—the part that goes over the ears and is attached to the bit; the reins—leather straps held by the rider that connect to the bit; and the bit—the piece that goes into the mouth of the horse, and to which the headpiece and the reins are attached. As you can see, everything connects to the bit, which is how you communicate directions while riding.

There are an overwhelming number of bits to meet various purposes, but the one right for your horse is the simplest and kindest bit. It should be the mildest bit that facilitates communication with your horse. It may take some experimenting to decide what works best. Your horse may do well with the snaffle bit, the most common type of bit, or the curb bit, used mainly in Western riding.

If your horse is bit chomping, tossing his head, stiffening his jaw, or hanging his tongue out, he may be trying to tell you his bit doesn't fit and is uncomfortable. It may not be suited to the shape of his mouth or dental condition.

ADDITIONAL TACK

Extra padding is used beneath the saddle to absorb sweat (and prevent the saddle from slipping), to keep the underside of the saddle clean, and for additional comfort for your horse. Popular options include a saddle cloth or a numnah, with the main difference being that the latter is cut in the shape of a saddle.

Turnout rugs are used to provide warmth when in pasture. Rainsheets provide protection from wind and rain. Fly rugs are used to keep flies away. Coolers are rugs used to protect the horse from cooling while wet, and to wick moisture away from his coat.

HORSE CARE

DAILY NEEDS

Many horse owners pay for their horses to be cared for by a third party—something known as boarding. This is a good solution for those who don't have the ability to care for their horses from home, due to space or time constraints. The boarding facility may take care of food, shelter, and turnout daily, leaving the owner to ensure the horse is well exercised. Other horse owners provide full care for their horse themselves, and it can be a formidable—and fulfilling—responsibility.

Routines will vary, but all who care for horses will agree that it is a significant amount of work. And it is a 365-day-a-year job. Holidays or not, the horse still needs to be fed, turned out to pasture, tacked up, exercised, and groomed. Stalls need to be mucked out and tack needs to be cleaned. Dark, cold mornings, or days when you crave just one more hour of sleep, the horse is waiting. It's not a commitment to enter into lightly, but the fact that so many successfully take on the responsibility, and enjoy the time spent in the stable, speaks to the intrinsic and tangible rewards of sharing your life with a horse.

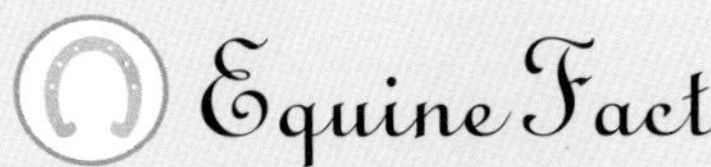

A daily health check should be performed while grooming to prevent problems and catch any existing issues early (see chapter 16).

DAILY ROUTINE

If you plan to care for your own horse, and you're not yet an early morning person, you will become one. Most people responsible for horse care are at the stable by 5:30 to 6:00 am to mix their horse's feed or fill haynets (slow feeders for hay) if needed. Then it's time to feed the horse and provide fresh water. The horse will generally be rugged up following feeding, weather dependent, and turned out to pasture. Generally this is when the stall is mucked out. After a few hours minimum in pasture, the horse will usually be brought in and brushed. At some point during the day the horse will need to be exercised for up to two hours. He will need to be tacked up prior to riding and untacked after (see chapter 13). Grooming is done before and after riding (see chapter 15). The next feed will be late afternoon or early evening and then, weather dependent, the horse will again be rugged up. Most horse owners who stable the horses on their own land will also check once more on the horse before bed. It's a long day, but necessary unless you are boarding your horse at a stable that handles much of the daily care.

BEHIND THE SIGNS

Daily Exercise

All horses, but particularly stabled horses, need regular exercise to remain happy and healthy. Riding provides the best exercise and should be in addition to the time the horse spends grazing. Without daily exercise, most horses will get into mischief or act up to release pent-up energy, or they may develop stable vices. In both scenarios, your relationship will be weakened.

FEED

Individual horses have different nutritional needs, depending on factors such as lifestyle and age. It may be hay, which is made up of a mixture of dried plants. It's nutritious, provides roughage to aid digestion, and keeps horses chewing (one of their favorite activities). There are different types of hay available, falling under either legumes or grasses, and some are better for putting on or losing weight. Your horse's health and lifestyle will determine what is best for him, a decision your veterinarian can help you with. Hay cubes are also an option; they are concentrated, offering all the good stuff of baled hay but requiring less chewing. Pellets are also a concentrated feed, most often used as a supplement. Bran is well received by horses, but should be given weekly rather than daily. Grain is a popular feed, generally best for very active horses. Pasture, complemented by other feed when necessary, allows plenty of grazing time. As you can see, there are many feed choices, with one, or a mix, the answer to your horse's specific needs. Except when at pasture, a feeder is recommended to prevent your horse from ingesting anything from the ground that he shouldn't, and that could cause health

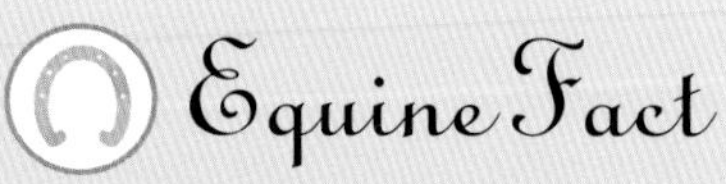

Treats can either be hand-fed to your horse, or you can use a feeder. If your horse pushes or crowds you to get at the treat then a feeder is recommended.

problems such as colic. Your horse should also have regular access to a mineral salt block that he will lick to get the salt and minerals required. Treats, such as red apples or carrots, should also be given daily.

Exercise: This is a must, every day. It should be in addition to time spent in pasture. At a minimum it should be at least half an hour a day, but up to two hours is recommended, depending on your horse's lifestyle and age. All horses benefit from exercise, even older ones as it helps keep them limber. Exercise may be made up of a combination of hacking and schooling, and the occasional longeing (also known as lungeing), whereby the horse is not under saddle but works from the end of a long line to respond to commands). Exercise will depend on the goals of the horse owner and the discipline or activity they are involved in.

Mucking out: Another must, every day. The amount of waste your horse produces each day is substantial, and if you don't clean up after him it will smell, attract flies and other parasites, and cause health problems. Manure should be scooped and removed by wheelbarrow to the muckheap, located away from the stables. Wet bedding—whether wood shavings, pellets, or sawdust—will clump. Remove this by fork or shovel and top bedding up with fresh bedding. Manure in pasture should also be removed, either daily or weekly. Check your area for the rules regarding legal equine waste disposal.

WEEKLY, MONTHLY, AND YEARLY ROUTINE

Water trough and feed buckets should be scrubbed clean each week to avoid any buildup. Fences should be checked to make sure they are in safe working order, with no protruding nails or wire that could cause injury. Feed and bedding supplies should be checked to ensure you have a two-week supply on hand. General barn or stable management tasks, such as checking and, if needed, clearing drains, should be completed.

Every six weeks your horse's hooves will need to be trimmed and if he is shoed, you'll require a farrier to reset. Every two or three months your horse will need to be given deworming medication. Every six months the stall should be cleaned thoroughly with a bleach and water solution. Yearly your horse will need veterinary checkups including immunizations, and he may need to have his teeth floated.

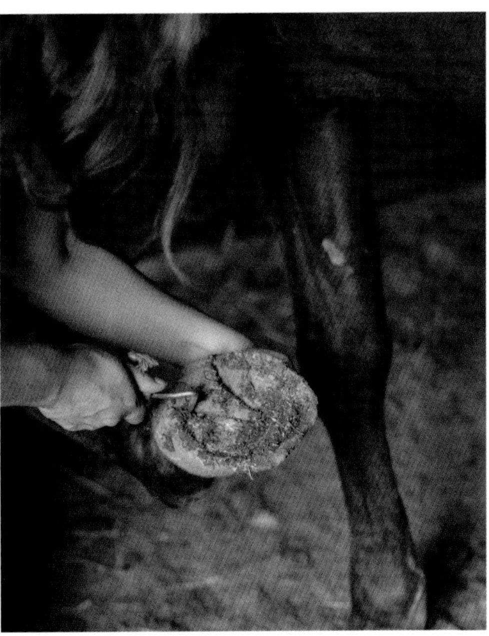

No. 15

GROOMING BASICS AND EXERCISE

RESPONSIBILITIES AND CARE

"Do horses really need grooming? Wild horses seem to do just fine without it." In the wild, horses groom each other with their teeth, and it helps strengthen the bond between the two involved. Our domesticated horses rely on us for grooming. It not only helps your equine look and feel his best, it builds trust and enhances your relationship. Your horse becomes more comfortable and at ease with you, and this trust carries over to when he is under saddle, which improves your riding.

Regular grooming is also a perfect opportunity to check your horse from head to hoof. It will help you catch any red flags—swellings, rashes, abrasions, and more—that would otherwise be missed.

Before you begin to groom your horse, get all of your supplies together. Grooming doesn't have to be a time-intensive project, but if it's stop-and-go, with multiple trips into the tack room to get various supplies, it can become a chore instead of quality time for you and your horse. You may want to use a grooming pail to store your supplies and make it easy to carry them. Next, lead your horse to the area you'll be using to groom him and use a halter and crosstie to secure him. Make sure you have enough room, and he is not close enough to kick out at another horse. You're now ready to begin grooming, starting with cleaning his hooves and finishing by thoroughly brushing his coat.

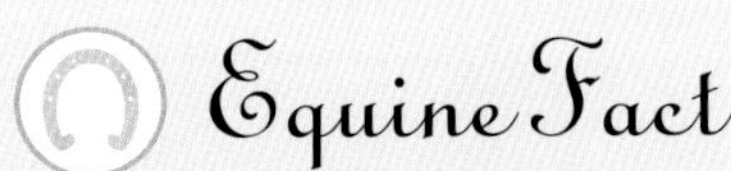

Grooming should be done before and after riding, and at least daily if your horse is not under saddle that day.

PICKING THE HOOVES

Helping your horse put his best foot, or hoof, forward, means picking his hooves daily. It can keep thrush (a fungal infection) at bay, and prevent an abscess or a crack in the hoof structure from worsening. Riding a horse that has a rock lodged in his shoe can lead to lameness, and take weeks to heal. Daily hoof cleaning can prevent that, and takes only minutes.

You will use the hoof pick to remove any irritants such as dirt, manure, shavings, and stones that may be pressing into the soles of the feet and causing discomfort.

To clean your horse's hooves:

Stand at your horse's shoulder, facing toward his rear. Bend your knees and run the hand that is nearest to your horse down the back of his leg to his foot. Use the command—usually "up" or "hoof"—that your horse is accustomed to. He should lift his leg at this point, but if he needs further encouragement, press your elbow into the crook of his knee. This should do the trick, at which point hold his lifted hoof firmly with one hand so that you can see the bottom.

Pick the foot out with the other hand, moving from heel to toe. Clean out the areas around the frog (the triangular area on the underside of the hoof). Remove all debris and check for any injury or abnormality. As you do this, keep your head well away from the hoof, as a precaution against a kick. When finished, gently place your horse's foot on the ground—never drop it—and move on to his other feet.

BEHIND THE SIGNS

Grooming Tools

There are a huge number of grooming tools to choose from, but the basics you will need to start include hoof pick, curry comb, dandy brush, soft-bristled brush, and assorted clean cloths. It's handy to store your tools in one portable place, such as a grooming pail or plastic toolbox. To keep your horse looking and feeling great, tools should be cleaned after each use and should not be shared amongst multiple horses so as to cut down on the spread of infections.

BRUSHING

This encourages horse health because it removes dirt from the coat, along with any parasites. It also releases the oils that provide luster to the coat, promotes good circulation, and provides a massage. There are three steps involved in this stage of grooming:

1. Currying your horse to loosen any dust and dirt: Begin at your horse's neck and work your way down his body, using the curry comb in circular sweeps. This will bring any dirt and dead hair to the surface. Avoid sensitive areas such as the head and below knees, as the curry comb is meant for the fleshier areas only. Every couple of strokes, knock the comb against a hard surface to release the dust.

2. Brushing to remove the loosened dirt: Using short, firm strokes, brush in the natural direction of your horse's coat using a dandy brush. Flick your wrist at the end of each stroke to pull dirt out, and every couple of strokes knock the brush against the curry comb to clean it. Avoid the head, and the area below the knees.

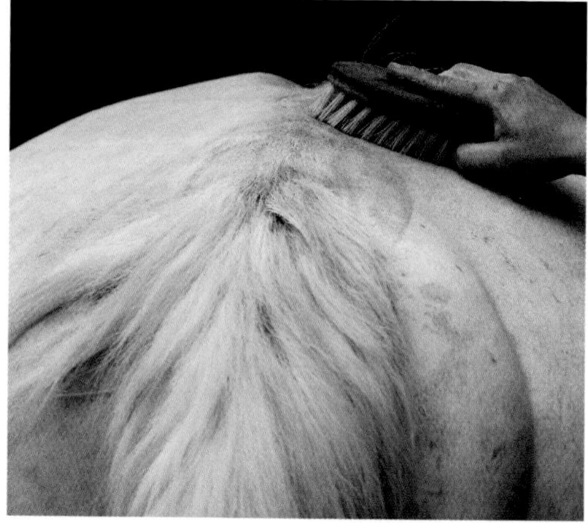

3. Polishing the coat: Use long, sweeping strokes and a soft-bristled brush (or a polishing cloth) to smooth the coat. As in step 2, flick your wrist at the end of each stroke to pull any remaining dirt or dead skin cells out, and clean the brush by knocking it against the curry comb every couple of strokes. Using the soft brush, you can also gently brush the face (taking care not to spook your horse) and below the knees. When you think you may be finished, run your fingers gently against the direction of the hair's growth to see if there is any remaining dust, and continue brushing until none remains. Pat down your horse.

If your horse flinches or you sense any discomfort while currying and brushing, decrease your pressure. Some areas are more sensitive than others, such as the shoulder bone and belly. Watch your horse's cues. His ears may be pointing to you throughout, but if they stiffen or flatten while facing back then your horse is telling you he is uncomfortable. The message is the same if his tail swishes in a quick back and forth continuous movement. Listen to what he is saying by being gentle in areas that are sensitive for him, and watching to see what he enjoys so you can repeat those actions. Brushing should be an enjoyable experience for your horse, and quality time for both of you.

GROOMING TIPS

- Keep your grooming pail out of the reach of your horse, to prevent him from chewing or stepping on it.

- Wear hard-toed shoes, in case your horse accidently steps on your foot. This is a common, but preventable, injury while grooming.

- Avoid quick, sudden movements that could startle your horse. Talk softly and keep a hand on him throughout grooming. This will calm him if needed, while also reminding him that you are there in the moments when grooming pauses, for example, when you move to the other side of your horse.

- When changing sides either walk far enough away from your horse or stay quite close to him; either method can help you avoid a kick. Avoid stepping over the crosstie, in case he startles and pulls back on the line.

- Never sit on the ground while grooming; instead, bend your knees when needed. If you have to move quickly it will be faster to move away from a squat position, whereas you would need more time if sitting.

ADDITIONAL GROOMING

MANE AND TAIL

Take a hands-on approach to detangling mane and tail. Use a generous amount of conditioner/detangling solution, and then finger comb to work away any knots or burrs. Finish by brushing with a soft-bristled brush, from the bottom up.

Tip: To help loosen snarls, saturate the hair in baby oil. Wait an hour, and then try to untangle the hair with your fingers. It should be easier to dislodge the burr or release the tangle, after which the oil should be washed out with horse shampoo to prevent buildup.

EYES, NOSE, AND DOCK

Use a damp cloth to wipe the eyes, nose, and dock (the area at the top of the tail). Reserve a separate color-coded cloth for each area to keep things sanitary.

Equine Fact

In the wild, horses groom each other, as well as rolling on the ground at will and rubbing against trees to maintain healthy skin and coat.

- Do not try to brush away wet mud. It should be either hosed off or left to dry, and then brushed away.
- Have a set of grooming tools for each horse, if possible, to prevent the spreading of contact diseases.
- Clean all tools thoroughly after grooming.

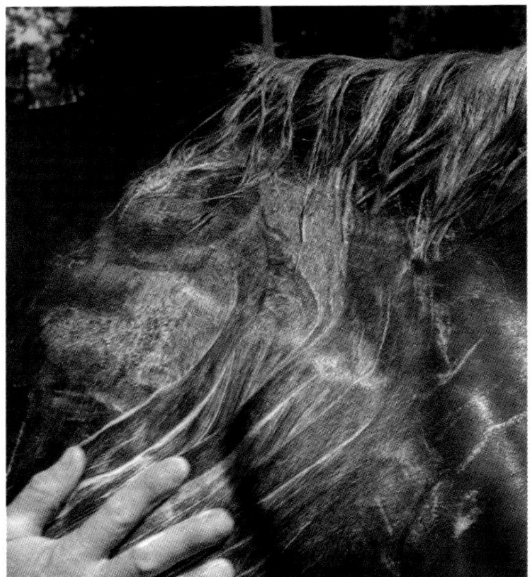

BEHIND THE SIGNS

Health Check

Grooming is a good opportunity to check your horse for any changes in condition that may indicate a health problem. While grooming, use your hand to feel all over your horse's body, legs, and hooves. Look for inflammation, abrasions, tenderness, and changes in coat or skin.

Each horse will have his own quirks and bumps, so it is only through regular health checks that you will be able to recognize when something is new or unusual, and may indicate a problem (see chapter 16).

No. 16

HOME HEALTH CHECK

REGULAR PREVENTATIVE CARE

Your horse can't communicate if something is wrong through words. In fact, horses often do not vocalize pain, a trait that helped keep them safe from predators in the wild. To protect and care for your horse you can learn to recognize the signs that indicate illness or injury, and incorporate a home health check into the daily grooming of your horse.

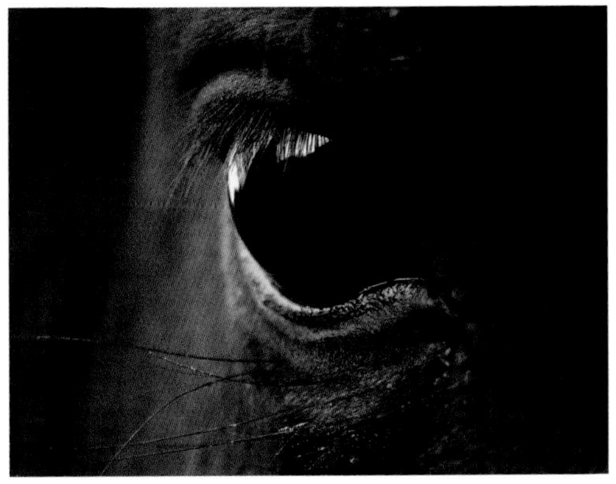

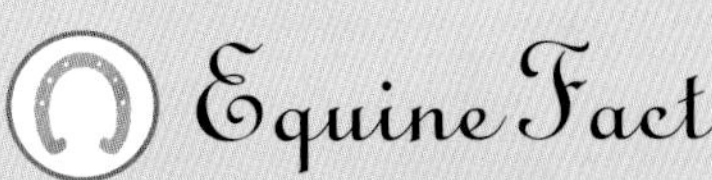

Corpora nigra are the brown or black shapes visible in the eye. They are common to horses, and are not usually an indicator of a problem.

HEALTH CHECK

Regular health checks help you recognize what is normal for your horse and what is not. Any change in behavior, such as decreased appetite or lethargy, or a change in appearance, could indicate a problem. Keep a record and share anything new or unusual with your veterinarian.

Your horse will need daily grooming, at which time you can perform a health check to look at:

Circulation. Do the capillary refill time test to ensure your horse's circulation is good, with the heart getting blood to all the tissues in his body. Press a finger gently but firmly on the soft tissue of your horse's gum and release. The spot where you pressed will become pale but should return to its pink color within four seconds.

Eyes, nose, mouth, and ears. Eyes should be bright and clear, with no swelling. Lids should be open and the membrane around the eye and inside the eyelid should be pink. There should be no excessive discharge from eyes or nose, or unusual smells from the nose and mouth. Nostrils should not be flared when the horse is at rest. Ears should be alert, following sounds.

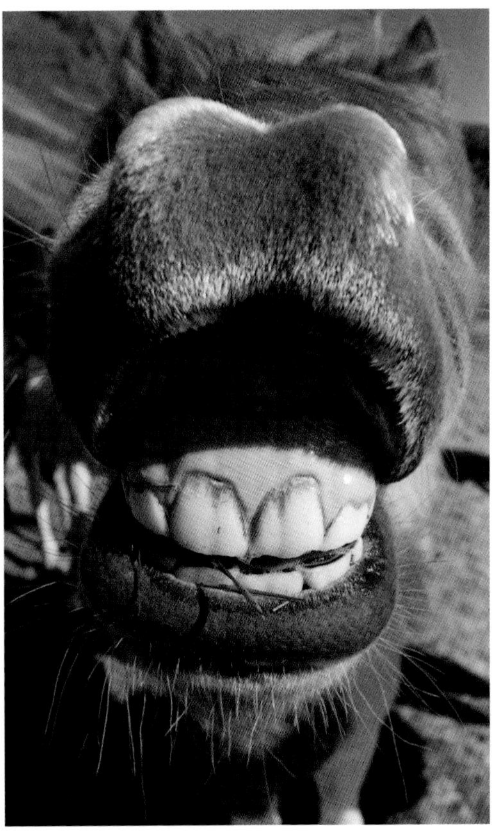

BEHIND THE SIGNS

Droppings Are a Good Indicator to Health

Droppings will vary according to diet, from the green cowpats or soft oval balls that result from eating spring grass, or harder ball-like droppings. Either way, there should be no fibrous lumps, and your horse should keep to a general schedule. Urine is generally strong-smelling and may be pale in color, or dark yellow, and cloudy.

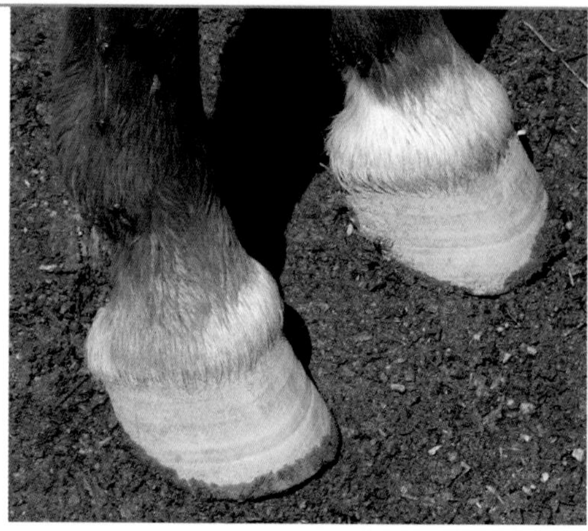

Feet. Hooves should be clean and free from rocks or any other items that may have lodged. There should not be any grooves or cracks in the hoof wall, or any splits at the bottom.

Skin, coat, and tail. Look for any lumps or bumps that have changed or are new. Check for swelling or hot spots. Either may signal a coat or skin problem due to allergies, parasites, infections, or a hormonal change. Check skin for dehydration by gently pulling a fold of the skin from your horse's neck. It should be supple and elastic. If he does not have enough fluids then his skin will not snap back in place immediately after you release it. The coat should be shiny, with no excessive shedding unless your horse is molting. His tail should be clean, without rubbed patches that indicate an irritant.

Pulse and respiration rates. Healthy rates vary from horse to horse, but in general pulse rate should be between 30 and 50 beats per minute, with a respiration rate of 8–16 breaths per minute when at rest. To check pulse rate place the tips of your fingers on the artery along your horse's lower jaw and count the beats. Respiratory rate can be established by counting the number of out-in movements of the ribs (each representing one breath) that your horse makes per minute.

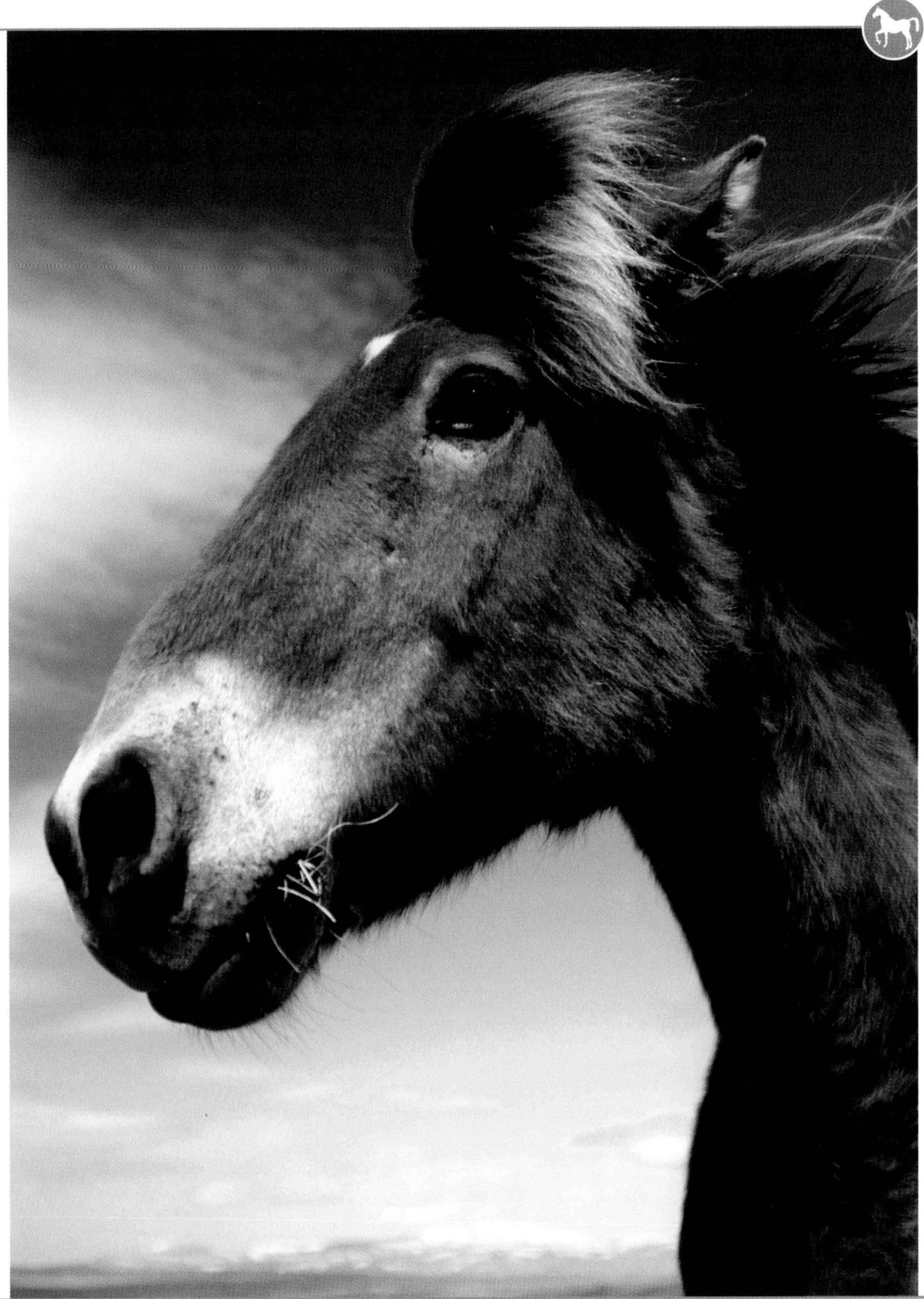

No. 17

HORSE HEALTH

RECOGNIZING AND TREATING HEALTH PROBLEMS

Knowing the common health problems horses experience translates to recognizing symptoms. This familiarity can prevent a minor problem from turning into a major worry.

Horses, being prey animals, don't normally make any sounds to show they are in pain. This trait has been passed down by their wild ancestors. It was an advantage to them, as they were able to hide weakness from predators. It's not, however, an advantage for domestic horses, since vocalization of pain might help identify problems. Since our horses can't tell us when something is wrong, owners must be very aware, and perform home health checks regularly (see chapter 16).

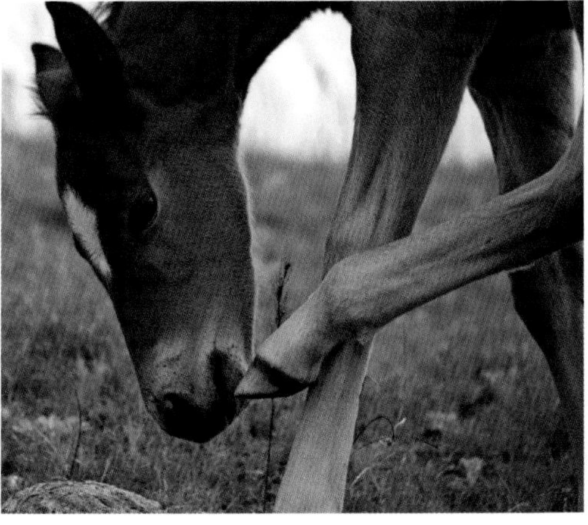

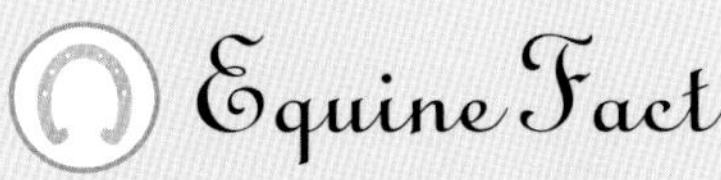

Equine Fact

The signs of lameness are easy to spot if you know what to look for; however, the site and cause may be best left to a veterinarian to decipher.

BEHIND THE SIGNS

Watch for Changes: Lameness

It's easiest to spot lameness when the horse is trotting. You may notice reluctance to put weight on one foot, the horse's gait may be off, and the horse may not be moving evenly. Most horses will experience lameness for different reasons at various times in their life but, if not treated, a minor problem can escalate quickly. Your veterinarian is the best person to diagnose the illness or injury, and prescribe treatment.

ARTHRITIS—DEGENERATIVE JOINT DISEASE (DJD)

WHAT YOU SEE:
Inflamed joints.

WHAT TO KNOW:
This is the most common form of arthritis, and it can affect young and old horses. Most often to be found in the hocks (ankles), followed by the knees. It may be a result of poor conformation, overwork, or old age. Prevention isn't always possible, but it's recommended you ensure that your horse is properly shoed, and do not overwork him. Intravenous supplements may also help. There are several treatment options, depending on severity.

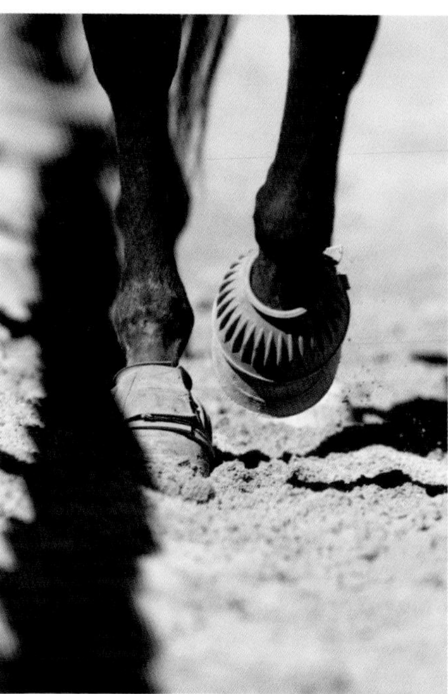

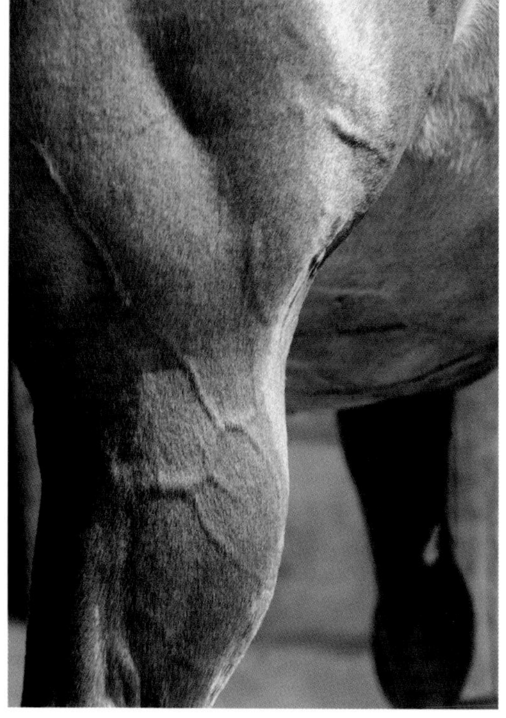

BOWED TENDONS

WHAT YOU SEE:
Swelling at the back of the leg. The lower leg may be sensitive and hot to the touch.

WHAT TO KNOW:
Caused by overexertion. An ultrasound by the veterinarian will determine severity. Treatment may involve anti-inflammatory drugs, icing, and rest to reduce swelling. Six months to a year of recovery will be needed, during which time exercise should be moderate and controlled.

CANCER

WHAT YOU SEE:
Lumps or tumors, most often on the eye, skin, or genital area. A change in appetite, energy, or temperament could also be a sign that something is wrong, perhaps a tumor on the internal organs.

WHAT TO KNOW:
A biopsy will be needed for diagnosis. If cancer is found then it may be treated in many different ways: surgery, chemotherapy, laser therapy, or radiation treatments.

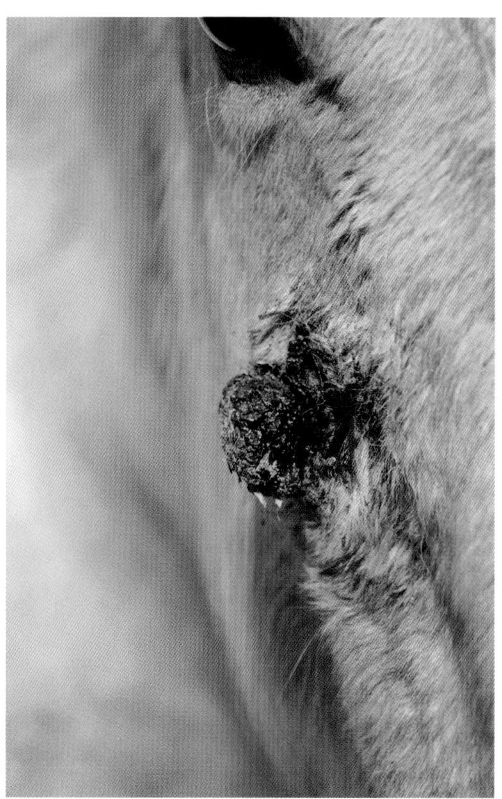

COLIC

WHAT YOU SEE:
Pacing or pawing, standing with legs stretched out, lying down, kicking at the belly, sweating profusely.

WHAT TO KNOW:
Colic refers to abdominal pain. It may be gas in the intestines, caused by a change of diet; a blockage of the intestines, caused by a foreign object; a twisting of the intestines; or gastrointestinal parasites. Although common, colic is also very serious. If you suspect your horse has colic, call the veterinarian right away. Treatment may involve medication or surgery. To prevent colic, feed your horse a proper diet of high-quality feed with plenty of fiber. Don't allow him to feed from the ground, where he might ingest dirt or other inappropriate materials. Ensure he has plenty of clean water available. Deworm regularly, and make any dietary changes gradually. Daily exercises with warm-up and cool-down are recommended. Professional dental care every six months or so is also important, as teeth problems can impede chewing and mastication of food, resulting in colic.

CORNEAL ULCER

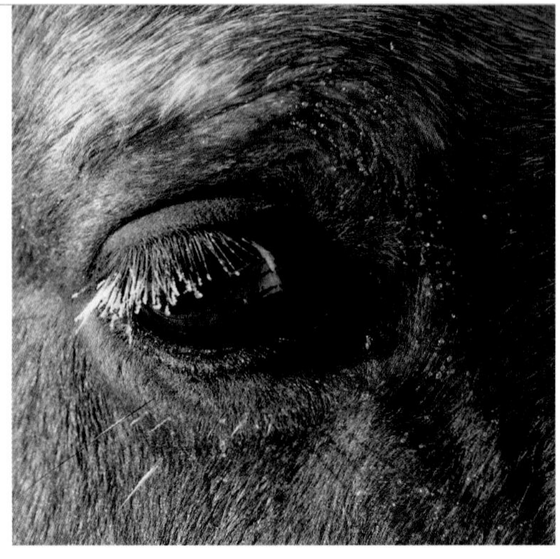

WHAT YOU SEE:
Squinting and tearing

WHAT TO KNOW:
Most horses will have a corneal ulcer, most often caused by a foreign body entering the eye and damaging the cornea, at some point. Although they are common, they can be become serious if not treated immediately. This is commonly caused when a horse has hung his head out of a moving trailer and had a small object fly into his eye as a result. Treatment typically involves a topical ointment prescribed by the veterinarian, to be applied multiple times per day.

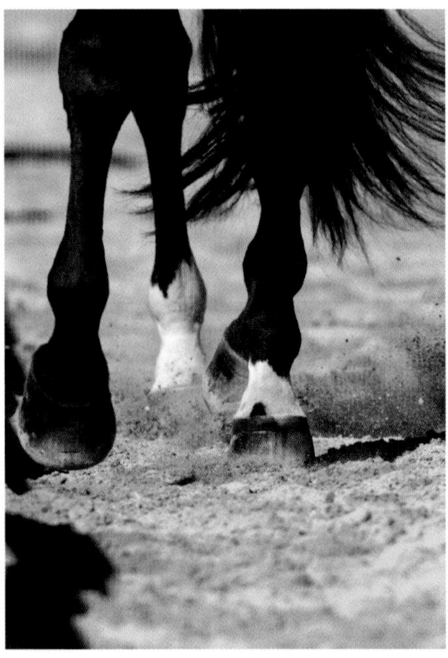

EPM (EQUINE PROTOZOAL MYELOENCEPHALITIS)

WHAT YOU SEE:
Uncoordinated and unusual limb movements, seizures, muscles in the face wasting away.

WHAT TO KNOW:
This is a relatively new disease, carried through the feces of opossums. To prevent it, keep feed from being contaminated by keeping it in containers, only feeding your horse from a trough or bucket, and washing feeders with soap and water regularly. It's easy to attribute lack of coordination to lameness, which could delay treatment. Your veterinarian may run tests, and may prescribe oral antiprotozoal medications.

ERU (EQUINE RECURRENT UVEITIS)

WHAT YOU SEE:
Inflammation, pain, tearing, sensitivity to lights.

WHAT TO KNOW:
ERU, sometimes known as moon blindness, is the number-one cause of blindness amongst horses, but treatment can prolong sight. ERU results from either damage to the eye, for example from injury and trauma, or disease, such as a parasite infection. Veterinarian treatment usually involves antibiotics or steroids to reduce the inflammation of the eye.

FLU

WHAT YOU SEE:
A mild case may involve a runny nose and lethargy, while in more serious cases the horse may experience a fever, runny eyes, appetite loss, stiffness, and coughing.

WHAT TO KNOW:
You won't catch the flu from your horse, but he is very contagious to other equines. Contact your veterinarian, who may provide antibiotics if needed. To prevent the flu, you can vaccinate against it, although this is not a guarantee of prevention, and during the fall and winter when it is going around you can try to keep your horse's contact with others to a minimum (such as making sure he doesn't drink from the same trough as other horses).

152

WHAT YOU SEE:
Decreased activity or appetite, irritability, diarrhea, and bouts of colic.

WHAT TO KNOW:
Gastric ulcers can be difficult to diagnose because the symptoms are easily attributed to other causes. For a definitive diagnosis, a veterinarian will perform an endoscopy. If diagnosed, treatment will involve feeding your horse frequently with a high-quality feed. It will also include plenty of time at pasture and a reduced level of training, as the stress of over-exercise is one of the more likely causes of gastric ulcers.

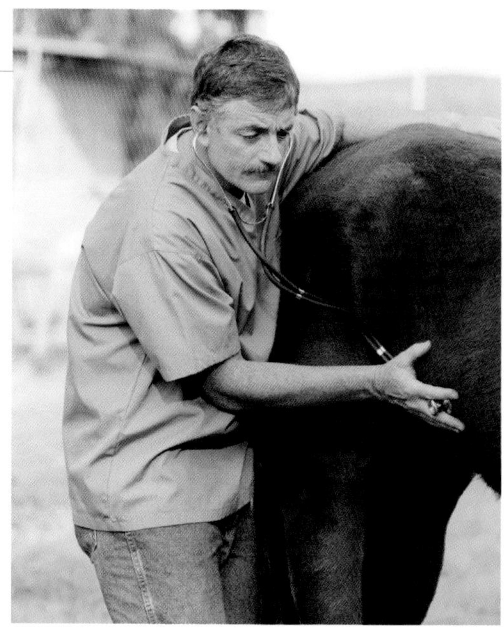

HEAVES

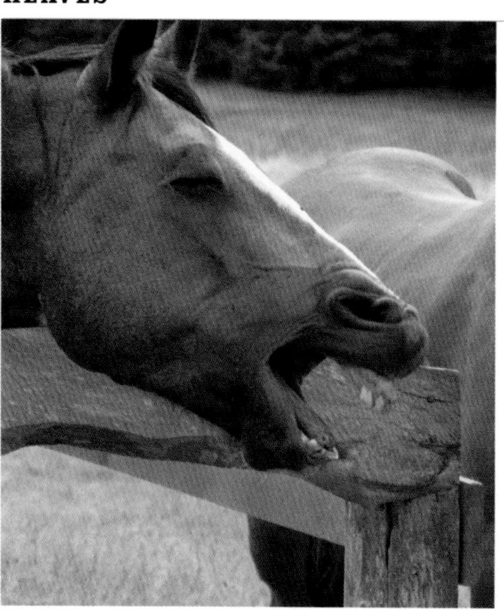

WHAT YOU SEE:
Difficulty breathing, coughing, and/or wheezing. The horse may have a "heave line," a prominent bulge of muscle along his ribs, caused by recurring heaves.

WHAT TO KNOW:
Also known as Recurrent Airway Obstruction (RAO), heaves are usually caused by airborne allergens such as dust, pollen, and mold. The best treatment is to keep your horse outside as much as possible, and to change his environment to avoid the causes. Eliminate sources of allergens, including any old hay and bedding. Depending on severity, treatment may also involve steroids or antibiotics.

LAMINITIS (ALSO KNOWN AS FOUNDER)

WHAT YOU SEE:
The horse may be walking with difficulty, he may rock back on his legs to shift his weight to a less painful position, he may lie down and refuse to walk.

WHAT TO KNOW:
Laminitis is a hoof disease, in which the coffin bone separates from the hoof. There are many possible causes: stress, such as trauma or surgery; eating too much grain; galloping on hard ground; reaction to drugs; trimming the feet too short; and untreated infections. Treatment may include: complete stall rest on very soft footing (deep shavings or sand), anti-inflammatory drugs, and cryotherapy (cold packs), for example. Laminitis is very serious; in worst-case scenarios, an affected horse can die.

Laminitis occurs most often in the front feet, although it can affect the hind feet as well.

PARASITES

WHAT YOU SEE:
The horse may be itching and rubbing his skin on objects. External parasites such as ticks, lice, and pinworms may be visible. In some cases, hair loss may be a symptom.

WHAT TO KNOW:
It may be impossible to rid your horse of all parasites, but they can be controlled through regular deworming. Prevention also includes regular removal of manure.

THRUSH

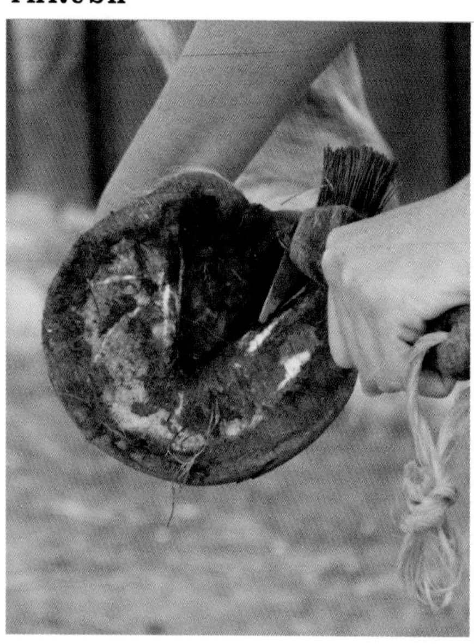

WHAT YOU SEE:
A black discharge on the bottom of the hoof. It will also be strong and unpleasant-smelling. There may also be deep grooves in the hoof.

WHAT TO KNOW:
Thrush is a bacterial infection that eats away at the horse's hoof tissue. Prevention includes daily hoof care. Left untreated it can result in lameness. Over-the-counter medication can be used in minor cases, with your veterinarian needed to treat serious cases. It's also a good idea to contact your farrier and book an appointment for the horse's hooves to be thoroughly cleaned and trimmed. To prevent thrush, clean bedding is a must. It will help keep hooves dry, and daily hoof picking will keep them clean.

TYING UP (ALSO KNOWN AS AZOTURIA)

WHAT YOU SEE:
The horse may be stiff with a shuffling gait; he may experience mild to severe cramps; he may sweat profusely; he may have an increased pulse and respiration rate; he may refuse to move; his urine may be discolored; and he may be unable to stand. Symptoms may occur during exercise.

WHAT TO KNOW:
A high amount of lactic acid in the body is the problem, but the cause is not known. It's believed that horses that are overworked, or work hard after a long rest, may be more likely to experience this. If your horse shows the signs, call your veterinarian immediately. To prevent tying up, your veterinarian may advice you to cut feed rations during periods of inactivity, provide supplements such as vitamin E, exercise daily and always warm up and cool down for a minimum of at least ten to fifteen minutes each.

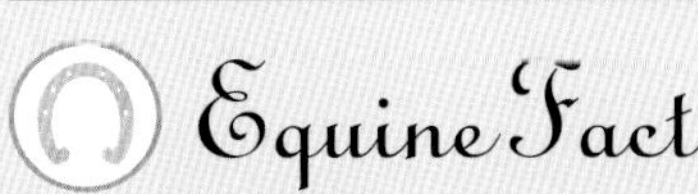

If your horse seems to seize up while you are riding, consult your veterinarian, as this may be a sign of tying up or azoturia.

No. 18

STABLE VICES

SIGNIFICANCE AND SOLUTIONS

Horses are social creatures. They are meant to graze, and they need exercise and stimulation. If they are isolated or confined for long periods of time, they can develop problem behaviors known as stable vices. These behaviors are often repetitive and can be difficult to stop once they develop into a habit.

Equine Fact

Horses are social animals that need human companionship as well as four-legged friends—whether a donkey, goat, or other hoofed animal—to thrive.

Horses learn how to behave by socializing with other horses. They learn what behavior is appropriate and what is not. Horses kept in isolation do not have the examples or companionship of others, and as a result often develop behavioral problems. Equines don't just want companionship, they need it. Without it they are off-balance, and compensate in ways that are not healthy. This weakens your relationship with your horse as well, because a horse that is so unhappy can't be at his best with you. He's also been let down by you, who he is dependent upon and trusted to look after his needs. Some stable vices that can occur include bolting feed, weaving, crib biting, wind sucking, and pacing.

BEHIND THE SIGNS

Toys to Entertain and Engage

All horses, but particularly stabled horses, need regular exercise to remain happy and healthy. Lack of exercise translates to unwanted behavior. Riding provides the best exercise, and should be in addition to the time a horse spends grazing.

The optimum amount and type of exercise depends on your horse's type, age, and temperament. Hotblooded horses are known for having a lot of energy and are bred to run. Coldblooded horses are generally workhorses—they're bred to pull farm equipment, but not necessarily to run for long periods of time.

BOLTING FEED

WHAT YOU SEE:
Horses that exhibit this behavior eat their food too quickly, without thoroughly chewing it. This can cause choking, or lead to colic. They do this for varied reasons. They may be hungry or they may feel stressed, particularly if there are other horses who they fear will take their feed.

WHAT TO KNOW:
More frequent meals should solve this problem, as once the horse is confident he won't go hungry he is less likely to bolt his feed. Some horses also react well when something is put in with their feed—such as a salt lick or medium-sized rocks. Although it may sound odd, this forces them to slow down as they eat because of the need to pick around the objects. You can also try spreading the feed flat, instead of using a bucket, as this will encourage the horse to take a step every bite or two, just as he does when grazing in pasture, and thus stop him from bolting his feed.

BEHIND THE SIGNS

The Theory Behind Stable Vices

It was once believed that horses developed stable vices by watching the behavior of other equines, but there is not enough evidence to support this. A current theory is that repetitive behavior such as weaving or crib biting releases natural morphine-like substances. These produce feelings of pleasure in horses, so they repeat the action. This is most often seen in horses who, given their environment, are unable to engage in natural equine activities.

WEAVING

WHAT YOU SEE:
Weaving is characterized by the horse moving his head repeatedly from side to side, usually over the stable door. Isolation and frustration are at the root of the behavior. An easier behavior to correct than most other stable vices, it is still one that should never occur. Like all stable vices, it's the sign of a horse that needs companionship, time to graze, and exercise.

WHAT TO KNOW:
Some fit a metal grill to the stable door to prevent weaving, while still allowing the horse to look outside the stall. But this does not get to the root of the problem. It can also cause even more anxiety in the horse, so it is not advised. Instead, plenty of time spent in pasture and, if possible, a bigger stall should prevent both weaving and pacing, resulting in a happier, healthier horse.

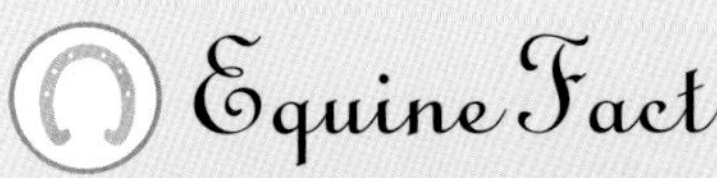

How much exercise Is enough? The best scenario is unlimited grazing for up to 18 hours per day. If this is not possible, expect to exercise your horse a minimum of two hours daily, divided between walking, riding, or grazing.

CRIB BITING AND WIND SUCKING

WHAT YOU SEE:

Also known as cribbing, crib biting occurs when the horse grinds his teeth on a solid object, grasping it in his mouth. He will usually choose what is right in front of him for this repetitive exercise, such as a post or the top edge of the lower stable door. This can cause significant damage to both the grasped object and the horse's teeth. Wind sucking is very similar to crib biting, except that while grasping an object with his teeth the horse will arch his neck and suck air into his stomach. This can cause the damage noted with crib biting, but may additionally cause digestive system problems.

WHAT TO KNOW:

Stop these behaviors at the start, before they become habitual. First, make sure the horse has plenty of mental and physical stimulation. Horses are not meant to be confined indefinitely, and need regular daily exercise with time spent grazing and under saddle. When they are kept for too long in a small space, whether paddock or box stall, horses can develop these vices out of boredom and anxiety, and these habits are much easier to prevent than break once formed.

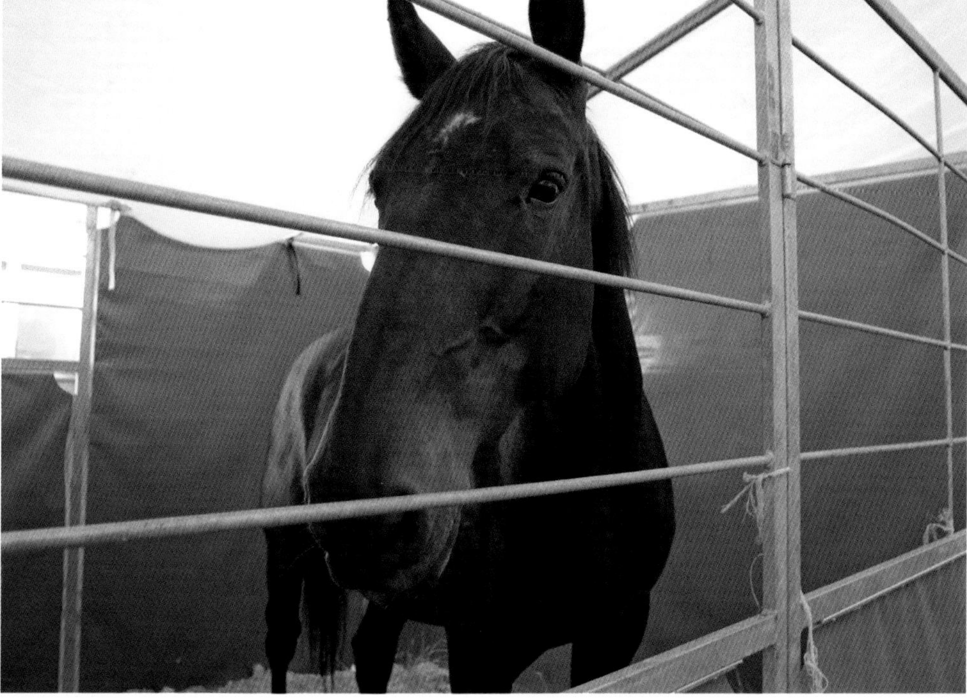

PACING (ALSO KNOWN AS CIRCLING)

WHAT YOU SEE:
This behavior describes a horse that walks endlessly within the space in which he is enclosed, usually his stall. Look out for signs of restlessness or unease—indications that your horse is agitated by some element of his surroundings.

WHAT TO KNOW:
Many of these behaviors share the same causes. Indeed, the reasons for pacing are typically the same as for other stable vices: boredom and frustration, brought on by being confined or isolated with a lack of stimulation. With minor changes to the environment in which you place your horse, solutions to the problems can be achieved simply. Although pacing is easier to curb than crib biting or wind sucking, given the right environment it should not develop.

No. 19

EQUINE FAQ

A GUIDE TO UNDERSTANDING COMMON QUESTIONS

Horses can be so intuitive—at times. They can be exceedingly friendly, or frustratingly aloof. In this way, they are just like people. Myths abound, and there are some aspects of equine behavior that are more commonly questioned than others. Why do horses sleep standing up? What would possess them to rush into a burning barn? Then there are the practicalities: How expensive is horse ownership? Why do we mount horses from the left? In this chapter, we look at some of the more enduring myths and the most frequently asked questions, along with their answers—straight from the horse's mouth.

WHY DO HORSES SLEEP STANDING UP?

Nature gave horses the great gift of being able to nap on their feet—perfect for the prey animal who might need to make a quick getaway. Their straight backs and considerable weight mean that they may lose valuable time if they first need to stand before fleeing. In case of danger, moving from an upright stance, paired with their speed, provides an advantage. They are able to nap while standing because their legs lock into place, preventing them from falling over even when completely relaxed and in nap mode. This ability is known as "stay apparatus," and it enables horses to stand for very long periods of time without tiring. It may not be immediately apparent when a horse in pasture is taking a standing nap, but look for relaxed ears along with a drooping head, neck, and lips.

Horses also lie down to sleep. In fact, foals take frequent recumbent rests during the first months of their lives. Adult horses may lie down to sleep for short periods of time, adding up to a total of an hour or so during the day, depending on factors such as their workload, diet, age, and the temperature. At night they instinctively rest standing up, an inherited trait from their wild ancestors, because this is when predators are more likely. The sleep phase of standing naps is of short duration as adult horses only need approximately three hours of sleep—made up of short naps—per twenty-four-hour period.

Sleep patterns vary amongst horses. Generally, if your horse is acting as he normally does and appears healthy there is nothing to worry about, but speak to your veterinarian if you have any concerns.

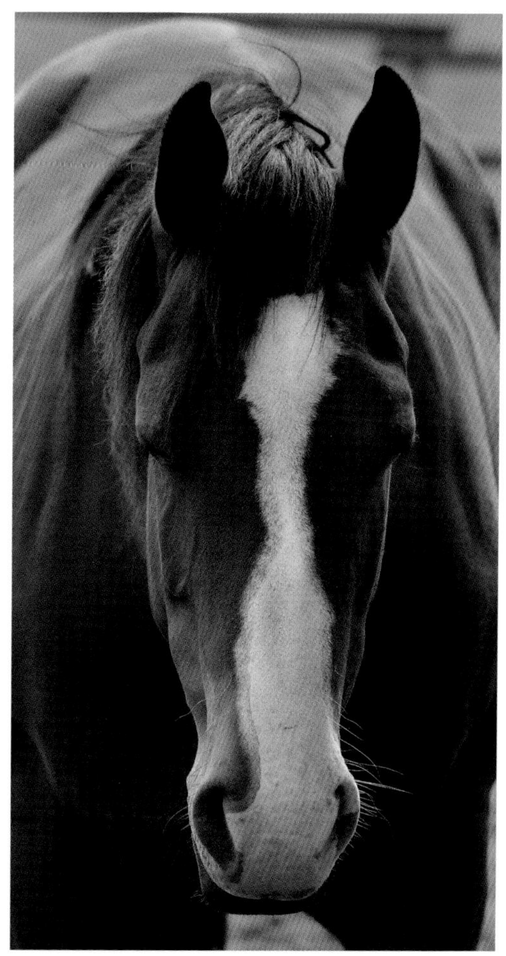

HORSES AND THE GLUE FACTORY?

Old or injured horses are not sent to the glue factory, to be used as an ingredient. This may have been true over a hundred years ago, but today it's simply a figure of speech that has endured. Many types of glue do use animal byproducts, but the myth of the aged horse being boiled down for glue can, thankfully, be put to rest.

FLIGHT OR FIGHT RESPONSE

A horse will instinctively flee at the first sign of suspected danger. As prey animals, their flight response enabled them to survive in the wild, with a sudden burst of speed helping them to outrun predators.

When cornered, a horse may fight, only because his option to flee has been thwarted. In these cases, aggressive behavior is the horse's reaction to a perceived threat.

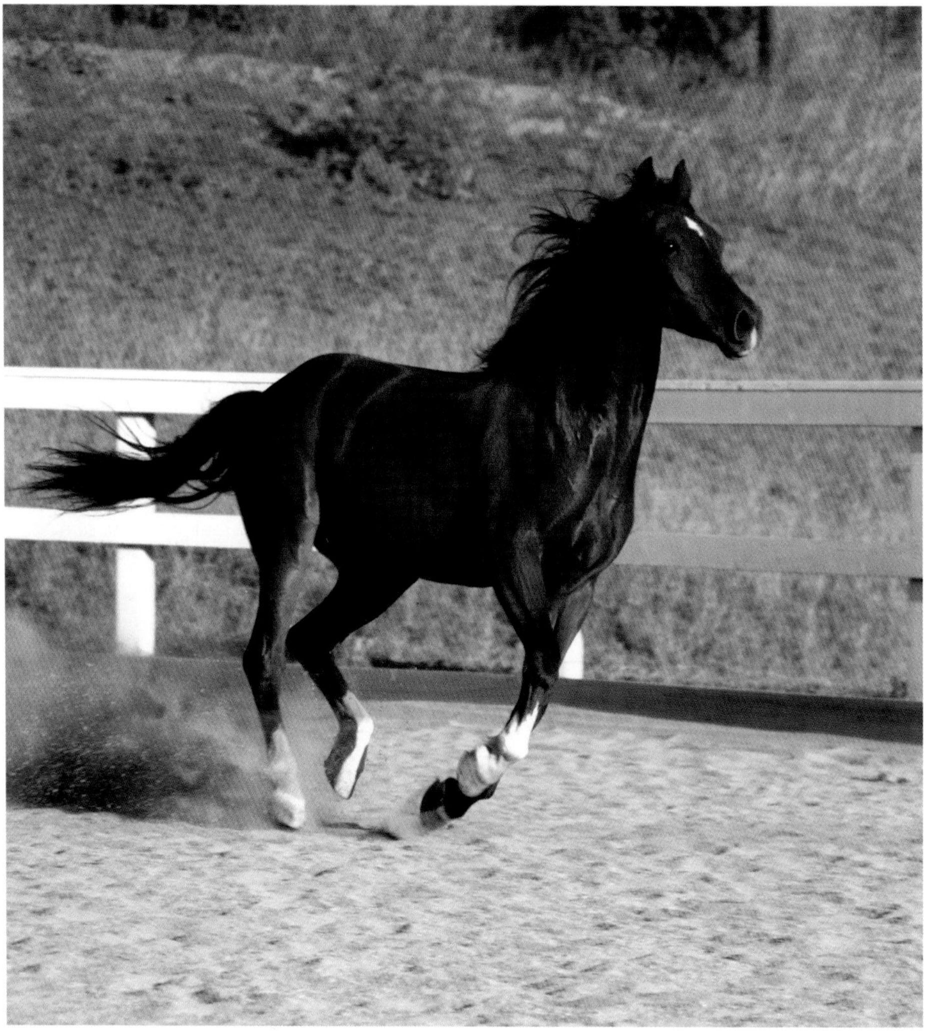

WHEN TACKING UP, DOES THE SADDLE OR BRIDLE GO ON FIRST?

Saddle first, then bridle. There are two main reasons for this: First, some horses will appear to expand in the belly when the saddle is put on, so doing this first gives them time to relax. By the time you have finished tacking up, their stomach should be back to normal—this is very important in order to tighten the girth properly. Second, if you bridle first you will need to tie the horse with his reins and this can be dangerous. It would be easy for the horse to step on a rein and then pull back, breaking the bridle and injuring his mouth. Or, if frightened, the horse might try to flee, injuring himself on the bridle and bit. Also, in the case of a fleeing horse the reins may easily snap. A halter and lead rope should be used to tie a horse; therefore always saddle first (see chapter 13).

BEHIND THE SIGNS

The Reality of Westerns

In the movies, cowboys throw or tie their reins around a hitching post when they want their horse to stay. Do the Westerns have it wrong?

The nature of a cowboy's work—for example, treating cattle in the middle of a range—meant there was often nowhere to safely tie their horse, or the time to tie their horse with halter and lead rope in emergency situations. These horses were well trained to stand and wait when tied by their reins, or even when the reins were simply dropped on the ground.

BEHIND THE SIGNS

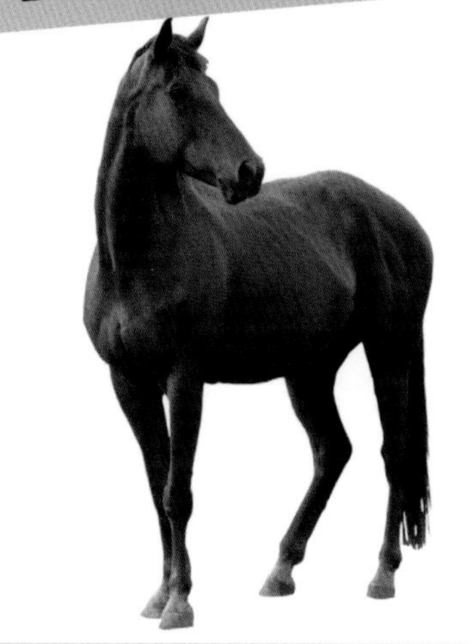

Healthy as a Horse

This saying is not one most horse owners would use! It must be based on the size and strength of the horse, because for such physically imposing animals their health can be temperamental. Regular care and grooming is necessary to keep the horse in good health. Even so, most horses will suffer an injury or illness at some point, but early detection and prompt veterinary care can help any health issues from escalating (see chapters 16 and 17).

WHY DO HORSES BLOW AIR ON EACH OTHER?

They're saying hello. They do this when they are reacquainted after a separation or when they meet a new horse. The smell of the other horse's breath is their identification, and how they will be remembered. This breathing of air onto each other when face to face also asks the question "Are you a friend?" Even without knowing horse "speak," the answer is pretty clear when observing horses as they make their introductions. The horse that responds with gentle blowing and perhaps some affectionate grooming of the other's coat is responding "Yes, let's be friends!" The horse that reacts with increased huffing indicates a need to establish rank. There are dominance issues at play, and the horse may proceed to bite or strike.

WHY ARE HORSES IN PASTURE OFTEN BLINDFOLDED?

What looks like a blindfold is most likely a fly mask covering the horse's eyes, muzzle, and possibly the ears. Made of a meshlike material, the fly mask has multiple functions. It protects against strong sunlight and air-borne irritants, such as sand and grit, while trailering or out in the field. As its name implies, it is also meant to keep insects away. Flies are attracted to the moisture in a horse's eyes, and can be a serious irritant since the horse can't simply brush them away. A fly mask provides some comfort and protection, while still allowing the horse to see out.

HOW MUCH DOES IT COST TO OWN A HORSE?

It depends, but it's recommended that you budget for at least one and a half times what your research tells you the costs will be. If you have a farm or a large lot of land then you may not need to pay stabling fees—one of the primary costs of horse ownership. Stabling fees vary widely depending on where the stable is located (close to urban areas, or far out in the country), and what they include (from pasture-only board to full-service stall boarding with daily turn-out for exercise and indoor arenas for riding in inclement weather).

If you are not stabling your horse, basic costs will include fencing and a barn or shed, bedding, such as shavings when stalling in cold or wet climates, feed (the quantity will depend on the horse's age, size, activity level, and the amount of pasture you can offer), and transportation, including a horse trailer or truck. Other basic costs all horse owners will have to bear include healthcare, which will cover veterinary procedures, such as immunizations, checkups, teeth floating, and emergency care, as well as owner-administered medicines, such as bimonthly deworming. Don't discount farrier (blacksmith) expenses, for regular trimming and shoeing, and the purchase and repair of tack, as well as equipment associated with grooming, feeding, and cleaning.

The financial outlay in purchasing a horse is small when compared to the upkeep needed. Costs differ according to geography and lifestyle—do your research by speaking to local horse owners, breed associations, and farmers, as well as veterinarians, farriers, and boarding facilities. But keep in mind that, although the joys of horse ownership are great, so are the costs, in time and money.

WHY WILL A HORSE RUN INTO A BURNING BARN?

This isn't a fact, although it's often repeated. There are some horses who, when panicked, may run into a burning barn. It may represent safety to them, as that is where they are stalled, especially as the horse can't understand fire or how destructive it can be.

WHY ARE HORSES SO EASILY SPOOKED?

It can seem quite counterintuitive to see such a powerful animal shy away from something we know to be harmless. But the point is that the horse doesn't know the object is harmless. As prey animals that have been historically low in the food chain, horses can be easily frightened by the unfamiliar. The horse may freeze, his head high, nostrils flaring and body tense, while staring at the object that has startled him. He may shy away, or back up from the object, or he may take flight—all of which could unseat a rider.

Most horses will relax once they have had an opportunity to thoroughly observe the object that has frightened them. If your horse will not calm down, lead him away from the object.

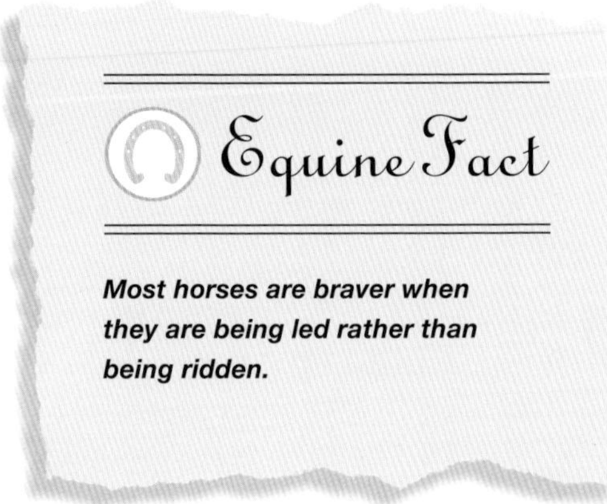

Most horses are braver when they are being led rather than being ridden.

Equine Fact

It's recommended that horses be taught to be just as comfortable with rightside, or "off side," tacking up and mounting as they are with left-side handling.

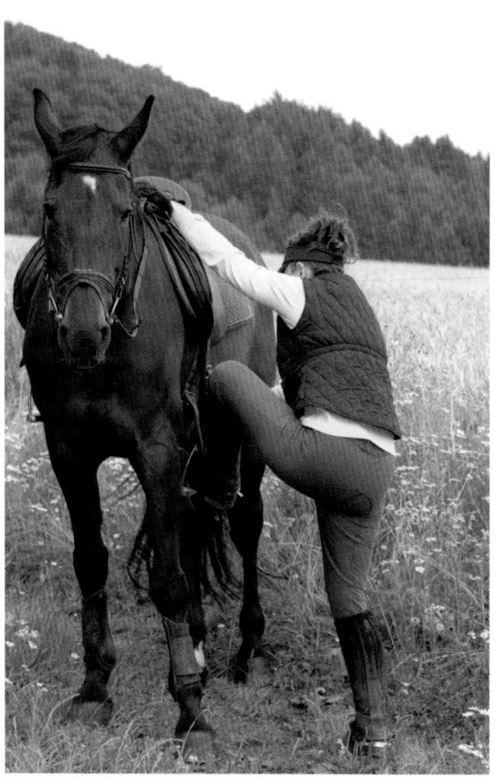

WHY DO WE MOUNT HORSES FROM THE LEFT?

Regardless of where in the world you are, you have likely been taught to mount your horse from the left or "near" side. This practice is based on tradition. When horses were first domesticated, their riders were most often farmers or warriors who carried tools or weapons. With most people right-handed, these items were typically worn on the left side so they could be drawn quickly and easily. Therefore it made sense to mount this way, to prevent the weapon or tool from dragging across the back of the horse. Mounting on the right would cause the item to hit the horse as the rider swung their leg over, likely causing the horse to bolt.

As a result of this practice, saddles, bridles, and other tack buckle from the left, or "near" side. For these reasons, mounting from the left has endured and continues to be taught in riding lessons.

WHAT DOES HORSEPOWER HAVE TO DO WITH HORSES?

Back when ponies were used to lift coal from mines, engineer James Watt coined the term "horsepower" to describe the amount of coal that one animal could pull. Based on his observation of ponies, he multiplied their output by 50 percent, to come up with an adult horse's capacity: 33,000 foot-pounds of work per minute. What this meant was that a horse working at one horsepower (HP) could pull 330 pounds of coal 100 feet in one minute, 33 pounds of coal 1,000 feet in one minute, or 1,000 pounds 33 feet in one minute.

This measurement was originally used to compare steam engines to draft horses in terms of power, but caught on as a unit of measurement that endures today when referring to power output and machinery.

ARE HORSES FRIENDLY ANIMALS?

Many first-time riders come away with this impression, particularly if their only riding experience is renting a horse by the hour. Unfortunately, these horses are simply reacting to their situation, as they are often poorly treated. Horses are also trained to respond to certain cues, but when forced to have numerous novice riders, these rental horses are often confused as to expectations. The popularity of horses worldwide is proof that they can be very friendly. Their mane may not wag when they see you, as a dog's tail will, but they will whinny at the approach of someone they trust, nuzzle them, and happily do their bidding given they are treated well.

No. 20

AGES AND STAGES

FOAL TO ADULTHOOD

Breed, environment, and the care a horse is given all factor into the aging process and life expectancy. Today, domestic horses typically live for between 25 and 30 years, with some reaching 40 years or more.

The stages of age differ between people and horses. As an example, horses typically walk just hours within their birth, something that would be quite miraculous in a human. At approximately 13 years a horse may be considered middle-aged, with an equine of 15-plus considered an older horse. However, each horse ages at its own rate, a result of many different factors such as genetics and lifestyle. Many horses of 15 years and older can still be found in competition today, with healthy pleasure horses capable of continuing regular activity well into their 20s. At one time, many horses would have been considered ready for retirement at 13 but the times, and medical care, have changed.

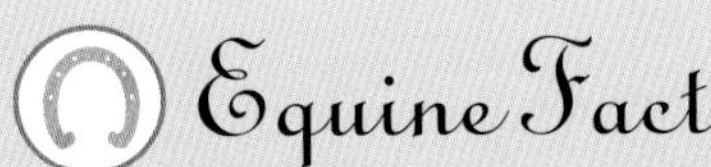

Smaller breeds have a longer life expectancy than larger horses, such as the draft breeds. Life expectancy is dependant primarily on breed and the level of care a horse receives throughout his life.

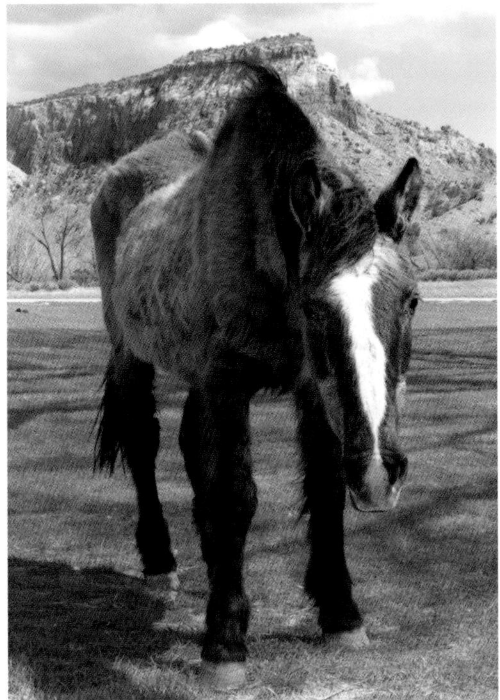

AT WHAT STAGE SHOULD TRAINING BEGIN?

Some experts believe this should happen from birth, using a process known as "imprint training." Others prefer to wait until the foal is a week old, believing the mare and foal need that time frame to bond, while the third camp prefer to wait until the foal has been weaned.

SIGNS OF AGING

Older horses typically have less energy. They may experience arthritis and weaker muscles, resulting in a gait that is not as smooth as it was. Their skin tone will become looser, their backs may sag, the hair around their muzzle and eyes may turn gray, and their appetite may change.

Regular veterinary care and exercise can prevent problems and keep your horse healthy as he ages. Exercise will help prevent muscles and limbs from stiffening and keep your horse comfortable.

TEETH TELL THE TALE

Although equine teeth grow continuously for many years, they are worn down by years of grazing tough grass and other foodstuffs. The angle of the teeth may also increase. This is why, although the surface of the teeth has been worn flatter with years, aged horses are sometimes described as "long in the tooth." Their angled teeth make the length from gum line to chewing surface longer. Although common in the past, many of the problems associated with aging teeth are now preventable with care and regular dental checks.

BEHIND THE SIGNS

Wear and Tear

Before equine dental care became routine, the life expectancy of the horse was much shorter. Years of grazing resulted in teeth that did not have the sharp edges necessary to chew and process the coarse grass stems that sustained them, so malnutrition and other health problems were more likely. The saying "don't look a gift horse in the mouth" reflects this. In those days, gifting a horse was more common and it was considered rude to look at the horse's teeth when being given one. This was because the teeth were a good indication of the horse's age, health, and value—almost the equivalent of asking the price tag. Today, our horses live longer, in part due to advances in dental care.

DEVELOPMENT AND MILESTONES

The development of horses varies according to breed and the care each horse receives.

Foals
Birth to One Year:

- Mares give birth after approximately 11 months of gestation.
- Upon birth, foals will stand and nurse within their first two hours.
- Foals will trot and canter within the first few hours and gallop within the first 24 hours.
- At birth, a newborn foal's legs are already almost as long as they will be as an adult, generally growing only approximately ten percent from birth to adulthood.
- Healthy weight gain for foals is up to three pounds, or over one kilo, daily.
- Socialization, through gentle handling and the introduction to new experiences, should start from a young age. In this way foals grow into well-balanced and curious adults, unafraid of new experiences.
- Roughly between days ten and 14, most foals show an increased interest, and appreciation of, their mare's feed.
- Basic horse training generally begins within the first month of a foal's life. Although too young to be ridden or driven, during year one they will gradually become accustomed to grooming, wearing a horse blanket, loading into a trailer, and being led by people.
- At approximately one month of age a farrier and/or veterinarian should check the foal's feet and limb conformation, to ensure the foal is developing as he should.
- From eight to ten weeks, supplementary feeding, to complement the mare's milk, is necessary.
- Domestic foals are generally weaned at between four and six months of age, although this varies between breed and discipline.
- Vaccinations typically begin at six months of age.
- At six to eight months of age, regular hoof trimming commences.
- From birth to 12 months of age, foals experience the most rapid development of their lives, attaining 50 to 60 percent of their mature weight and height within year one.
- During their first year, foals are less able to regulate body temperature, so they have a greater need for shelter during harsher temperatures than adult horses do.

DEVELOPMENT AND MILESTONES

Yearling to Colt/Filly *One to Four Years*:	• Yearlings (horses aged from one to two years) may be capable of reproduction at approximately 18 months, but are not fully mature physically. • Between one and two years of age, young horses can be unpredictable and full of energy, similar to adolescence in humans. • Male yearlings (colts) who will not be bred are typically gelded (castrated) as yearlings. • Skeletal structure continues to develop. Yearlings are too young to be put to work, although they may look physically strong enough. • By the age of two, foals attain 80 to 90 percent of their mature weight and height. • Aged four years and under, male horses are considered colts and female horses are fillies. • At three years of age, most horses begin training under saddle, although this is breed- and discipline-dependent. • Horses are generally considered mature at four to five years.

GLOSSARY

Aid: Signals used by the rider to pass instructions to the horse.

Bald: White or light color on a horse's head.

Bareback: Riding without a saddle.

Barefoot: Unshod.

Barn sour: Herd-bound; a bad habit that may result in a horse bolting back to the barn or to his herdmates.

Bay: A coat color ranging from tan to reddish-brown, with black mane and tail and usually black on the lower legs.

Bedding: The material used on the floor of a stall to absorb moisture and provide padding.

Behind the bit: When a horse draws his head in toward his chest to avoid contact with the bit.

Bit: A device placed in the mouth of the horse as a means of control. It is attached to the reins.

Black: A body color that is true black over the body, but may have white leg and face markings.

Blaze: White or light coloring on a horse's face, between the eyes from poll to nose.

Blemish: A visible defect that does not affect performance.

Blue roan: A body color that has a uniform mixture of black and white hairs all over the body.

Bolting: Eating very rapidly; gulping feed without proper chewing. Also, running away with rider.

Boots: Protective covering for the horse's hoofs and legs.

Bots: Parasitic flies.

Box: Boxstall; a four-sided stall to confine a horse.

Breed: A variety of horses consisting of a group that share the same genetic and physical characteristics.

Breed association: The organization that registers the birth and pedigree of a particular breed of livestock.

Breed character: The quality of conforming to the description of a particular breed.

Breeding class: Conformation class.

Brindle dun: A dun body color with darker streaks.

Broke: A horse that has been trained.

Broodmare: A mare used for breeding.

Browband: The topmost horizontal leather strap of the bridle that fits under the forelock.

Buckskin: A body color that is tan, yellow, or gold with black mane, tail, and lower legs.

Buckstitching: The decorative wide, white stitching used on Western saddles and bridles.

Bull pen: A training corral, also called a "round" pen.

Canter: A three-beat gait with right and left leads.

Cantle: The back of the saddle.

Chestnut: A color in which the body, mane, and tail are various shades of brown.

Chute: In cattle events, a fenced lane that contains a single cow behind a gate.

Cinch: Same as girth; used to hold saddle on.

Cinch strap: The strap of leather that is looped through the cinch to hold the saddle in place.

Colt: A young male horse that has not been castrated.

Conformation: Form and arrangement of the parts of a horse.

Coronet: The band around the top of the hoof from which the hoof wall grows.

Crossbred: Offspring of a sire and dam of different breeds.

Crossing: Breeding horses of different pedigrees.

Crosstie: A means of tying a horse in which a chain or rope is attached to each side of the horse's halter.

Cue: A signal, often made up of several aids, from the rider or handler that gives the horse instructions.

Curb chain: The chain attached to the bit passing under the horse's chin.

Curb strap: The leather strap on the bit passing under the horse's chin.

Curry comb: A device with many small teeth for cleaning hard-packed filth off a horse's coat.

Dally: To wind the rope end around the saddle horn.

Dam: Female parent.

Dandy: A medium-hard brush for grooming, used to remove loose hair and dirt.

Dappled: Rings or spots of different-colored hair on the coat of a horse.

Dock: The flesh and bone portion of the tail.

Double bridle: Bridle consisting of two separate headstalls and bits.

Draft horse: A horse of one of the breeds of heavy horses that was developed for farm or freight work.

Dun: A yellow or gold body and leg color, often with a black or brown mane and tail, and usually with a dorsal stripe and stripes on the legs and withers.

English: Referring to riding with English tack and attire.

Equitation: The art of riding.

Eventing: Combined training including dressage, cross country, and stadium jumping.

Far side: The horse's right side.

Farrier: A horse shoer.

Fault: Scoring unit to keep track of knockdowns, refusals, or other offenses.

Favor: To limp slightly.

Fender: Part of the Western saddle that protects a rider's leg from the rigging.

Fetlock: The tuft of hair on the back side of the fetlock joint.

Fetlock joint: Between the cannon and the pastern; the ankle.

Filly: A young female horse that has not produced a foal.

Flat: Class without jumping.

Flaxen: A golden mane or tail on a darker-bodied horse.

Flehmen: A behavioral response in which the horse's upper lip curls upward.

Float: To file a horse's teeth to remove sharp points.

Fly back: A bad habit in which a horse will suddenly pull back, often resulting in a broken halter or tie.

Flying change: A change of lead at the lope, without slowing to the trot.

Flying lead change: Change from one lead to another without changing gait.

Foal: A young, nursing horse of either sex.

Forelock: The hair growing between a horse's ears that falls on the forehead.

Fork: Part of the swells of a saddle that makes up the gullet.

Founder: Another word for laminitis, a serious disease affecting a horse's hooves.

Frog: Wedge-shaped pad in the sole of the hoof.

Gait: A specific pattern of foot movements, such as the walk, trot, and canter.

Gelding: A male horse that has been castrated.

Girth: A strap that runs around the horse's body to hold the saddle or harness in place.

Gray roan: A horse with a coat of mixed gray and white hairs.

Ground tie: To stand in one place, with reins dropped on the ground.

Ground training: When the trainer works the horse from the ground, rather than being mounted.

Grulla: A dun body color that ranges from bluish gray to brownish-gray.

Gymkhana: A program of competitive games on horseback.

Hackamore: A device to guide a horse without a bit.

Halter: Harness that fits over the horse's head by which it may be tied or handled.

Halter class: Conformation class.

Halter pulling: A bad habit in which a horse pulls violently backward on the halter rope when tied.

Hand: Four inches of height on a horse.

Hard keeper: An animal that requires more than the usual amount of food to stay healthy.

Haunches: Hindquarters.

Head shy: Description of a horse who shies away from having his head touched.

Header: In team roping, this rider ropes the steer's horns.

Headstalls: Another term for bridles.

Herd-bound: When a horse is too dependent on being with other horses and doesn't want to be separated from them.

Hoof: The hard horny covering of the horse's foot.

Hoof pick: A metal one-tined rakelike tool, used to clean debris from a horse's hoof.

Horn: The highest part of the pommel, on the western saddle. Used to dally a rope.

Hotblood: A horse of Thoroughbred or Arab breeding.

Hunter: A type of horse, not a breed, which is suitable for field hunting or show hunting.

In-and-out: A combination fence.

In-hand class: A class in which the horse is led by the exhibitor.

Irons: Stirrups on an English saddle.

Jog: A slow Western trot.

Jumper: A horse judged on jumping performance.

Lameness: Unevenness in the horse's stride when moving.

Laminitis: Inflammation of the horse's hoof.

Latigo: The cinch strap on a Western saddle.

Lead change: A change from one lead to another with a walk, trot, or halt in between.

Long trot: An extended jog or trot.

Longeing (Lungeing): To work a horse from the ground, using a line.

Mare: Mature female horse.

Martingale: A piece of training equipment designed to fix a horse's head in position.

Muzzle: The end of a horse's face, including the nose, nostrils, and lips.

Neck rein: Movement of the rein against the horse's neck that cues him to turn.

Offside: The horse's right side.

Pacing: Continuous stall or pen walking.

Paddock: A small pasture.

Paint: A breed of horse with large blocks of white and black or white and brown coat color.

Palomino: A breed of horse that has a golden body color and a light to white mane and tail.

Pastern: The area and joint between the fetlock and hoof.

Pedigree: A listing of a horse's ancestors.

Pelham bit: A combination of snaffle bit and curb bit requiring two reins.

Pen: The show ring or an outdoor living space.

Performance horse: A horse especially accomplished in showing, jumping, and dressage.

Pommel: The wide uplifted front of the saddle.

Post: To rise from the saddle in rhythm with the horse's trot.

Purebred: A horse with both sire and dam of the same breed.

Rearing: A bad habit in a horse that describes the raising up on hind legs when being led or ridden.

Red roan: A mixture of red and white hairs all over a horse's body.

Registered: A horse of purebred parents that have numbered certificates with a particular breed organization.

Rein: The long strap that passes from the bit to the rider's hands, used to control the horse.

Rigging: The saddle straps that connect the cinch and the saddle tree.

Roan: A horse color resulting from a mixture of white and black or white and red hairs.

Rug: A horse blanket.

Run: A long, narrow fenced-in area.

Sclera: The area of the eye surrounding the cornea.

Seat: The part of the saddle where the rider sits, or the way a rider sits in a saddle.

Sire: A male parent.

Skirt: The square or round leather flaps under the saddle seat.

Sock: White above the fetlock.

Sorrel: A reddish or copper-red coat.

Sound: Having no defect, visible or unseen, that affects performance.

Stable vice: Abnormal behavior in the stable environment.

Stallion: A male horse four years of age and over (not gelded).

Stirrup: Part of the saddle used to support the rider's feet.

Stocking: A white leg marking above the cannon.

Strangles: A bacterial respiratory disease.

Stripe: A white streak down the face.

Swells: The exterior projection of the fork of a saddle.

Tack: Equipment used on a horse.

Temperament: The general consistency of a horse's behavior.

Thrush: A disease of the hoof.

Tobiano: A Paint and Pinto coat pattern of spots.

Tree: The basic framework of the saddle.

Trot: A two-beat diagonal gait.

Unsoundness: A defect that may or may not be seen but that affects performance.

Weaving: Rhythmic swaying of weight from one front foot to the other when confined.

Western: Referring to riding with Western tack and attire.

Wind sucker: Cribber; a horse that holds an object with his teeth and sucks in air.

Withers: The highest part of the horse's back, where the neck joins the back.

Yearling: A male or female horse or pony that is one year old.

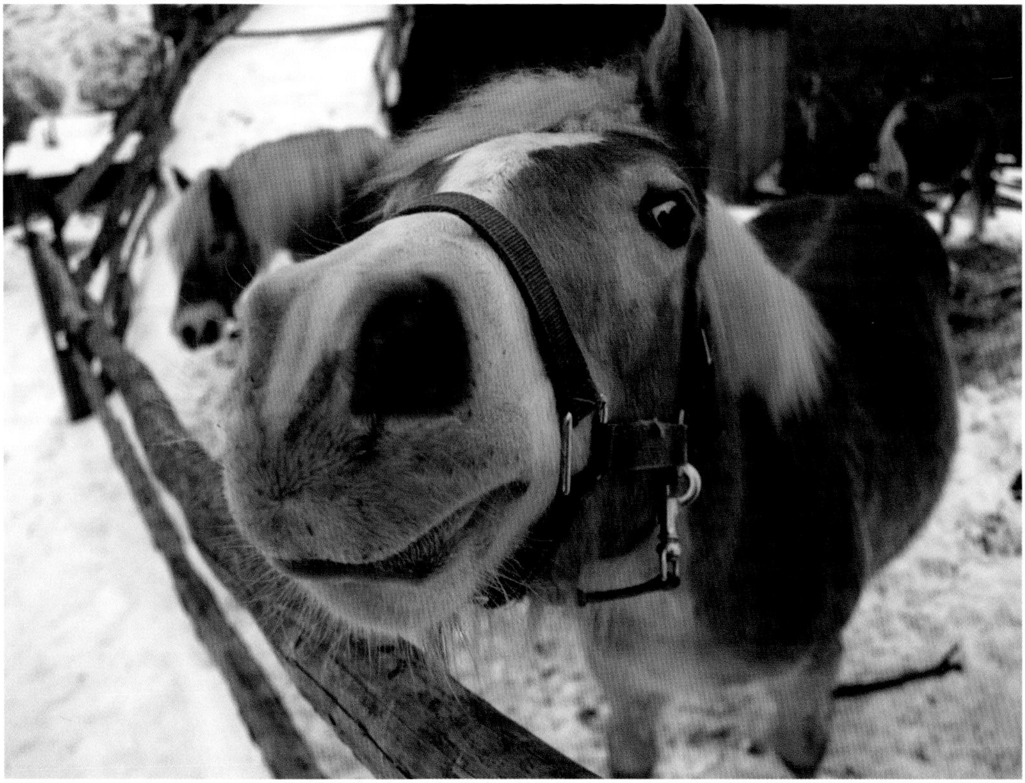

PICTURE CREDITS

Page 8	Andrielle | Dreamstime.com
9	Siloto | Dreamstime.com
10 Left	Websubstance | Dreamstime.com
10 Right & throughout	Fouroaks | Dreamstime.com
11	Zagorodnaya | Dreamstime.com
12	Panaroid | Dreamstime.com
13	Res2500 | Dreamstime.com
14	Iofoto | Dreamstime.com
15	Edoma | Dreamstime.com
16	Filmfoto | Dreamstime.com
17	Ninetteluz | Dreamstime.com
18	Maryart | Dreamstime.com
19	Hkuchera | Dreamstime.com
20 Left	Razihusin | Dreamstime.com
20 Right	Dvernytska | Dreamstime.com
21	Ciprian.d | Dreamstime.com
22	Lincolnrogers | Dreamstime.com
23	Afhunta | Dreamstime.com
25 Left	Hkuchera | Dreamstime.com
25 Right	Afhunta | Dreamstime.com
26	Isselee | Dreamstime.com
27 Left	Leaf | Dreamstime.com
27 Right	Fotorvr | Dreamstime.com
28	Cynoclub | Dreamstime.com
29 Right	Laksen | Dreamstime.com
29 Left	Cathyclapper | Dreamstime.com
30	Shawnjackson | Dreamstime.com
31	Cynoclub | Dreamstime.com
32	Jjwalker | Dreamstime.com
33	Fotovitaly | Dreamstime.com
34	Kurhan | Dreamstime.com
35 Left	Justplainphotos | Dreamstime.com
35 Right	Intst | Dreamstime.com
36 Left	Druzkate | Dreamstime.com
36 Right	Corolanty | Dreamstime.com
37 Left	© Zuzule | iStockphoto.com
37 Right	Dozornaya | Dreamstime.com
38 Top-right	Dinozzo | Dreamstime.com
38 Bottom-right	Framed1 | Dreamstime.com
38 Bottom-left	Kumabear | Dreamstime.com
39	Shiningcolors | Dreamstime.com
40 Left	Jimsphotos | Dreamstime.com
40 Right	Leaf | Dreamstime.com
41 Left	Krzyssagit | Dreamstime.com
41 Right	Wendibcr | Dreamstime.com
42	Mikle15 | Dreamstime.com
43	Jdebordphoto | Dreamstime.com
44 Right	Marilyna | Dreamstime.com
44 Left	Jeffbanke | Dreamstime.com
45	Pixrgb | Dreamstime.com
46 Top-right	Victoriiabaliura | Dreamstime.com
46 Bottom-right	Bfegert | Dreamstime.com
47 Left	Stevesimages | Dreamstime.com
47 Right	Tristana | Dreamstime.com
48	Nastenok | Dreamstime.com
49	Static85 | Dreamstime.com
50 Number 1	Pontuse | Dreamstime.com
50 Number 2	Sfmorris | Dreamstime.com
50 Number 3	Burr | Dreamstime.com
50 Number 4	Mschalke | Dreamstime.com
50 Number 5	Allx | Dreamstime.com
50 Number 6	Zandebasenjis | Dreamstime.com
50 Number 7	Nastenok | Dreamstime.com
51 Number 1	Agorafobia | Dreamstime.com
51 Number 2	Olikit | Dreamstime.com
51 Number 3	Susann1 | Dreamstime.com
51 Number 4	Wildhorsedesigns | Dreamstime.com
51 Number 5	Bjakko | Dreamstime.com
51 Number 6	Olikit | Dreamstime.com
52 Number 7	Nastenok | Dreamstime.com
52 Number 8	Brookhouse | Dreamstime.com
52 Number 9	Regatafly | Dreamstime.com
52 Number 10	Tamarabauer | Dreamstime.com
52 Number 11	Ellende | Dreamstime.com
52 Number 12	Wildhorsedesigns | Dreamstime.com
52 Number 13	Regatafly | Dreamstime.com

53 Number 1	Dizajune | Dreamstime.com
53 Number 2	Ctmphotog | Dreamstime.com
53 Number 3	Volare2004 | Dreamstime.com
53 Number 4	Oksix | Dreamstime.com
53 Number 5	Djk | Dreamstime.com
54 Number 1	Susann1 | Dreamstime.com
54 Number 2	© Christa Brunt | iStockphoto.com
54 Number 3	Alex0364 | Dreamstime.com
54 Number 4	© lindarocks | iStockphoto.com
54 Number 5	Shhaase | Dreamstime.com
55	Tristana | Dreamstime.com
56	© Fonetix | Dreamstime.com
57	Megalomaniac | Dreamstime.com
58	Tomashko | Dreamstime.com
60 Left	W.kaveney | Dreamstime.com
60 Right	Ankevanwyk | Dreamstime.com
61	Wrennie | Dreamstime.com
62	Isselee | Dreamstime.com
63	Lammeyer | Dreamstime.com
64	Actionsports | Dreamstime.com
65 Left	Enjoylife25 | Dreamstime.com
65 Right	Shvetic | Dreamstime.com
66	Bjakko | Dreamstime.com
67	Lunamarina | Dreamstime.com
68	Canettistock | Dreamstime.com
69	Corolanty | Dreamstime.com
70 Top	Studioceja | Dreamstime.com
70 Bottom	Pinkbadger | Dreamstime.com
71 Top	Madeinmsu | Dreamstime.com
72	Cynoclub | Dreamstime.com
73 Top	Enruta | Dreamstime.com
73 Bottom	© bermau | iStockphoto.com
74	Jeffbanke | Dreamstime.com
75 Left	JustinShootme | Dreamstime.com
75 Right	Marekuliasz | Dreamstime.com
76 Top	Lunamarina | Dreamstime.com
76 Bottom	Cringuette | Dreamstime.com
77	Fouroaks | Dreamstime.com
78 Top	Krystof | Dreamstime.com
78 Bottom	Christiankieffer | Dreamstime.com
79 Top	Mokreations | Dreamstime.com
79 Bottom	Aremac | Dreamstime.com
80	Shuksrphoto | Dreamstime.com
81	Christiankieffer | Dreamstime.com
82 Top	Mokreations | Dreamstime.com
82 Bottom	Galantnie | Dreamstime.com
83	Leaf | Dreamstime.com
84	Djk | Dreamstime.com
85	Olgaru79 | Dreamstime.com
86	2circles | Dreamstime.com
87	Novic | Dreamstime.com
88	Djk | Dreamstime.com
89 Top	Elenathewise | Dreamstime.com
89 Bottom	© Chris Fertnig | istockphoto.com
91	Bsauter | Dreamstime.com
92	Allenfive5 | Dreamstime.com
93	Liquidphoto | Dreamstime.com
94	Cloudbow | Dreamstime.com
95	Intst | Dreamstime.com
96 Top	© nullplus | iStockphoto.com
96 Bottom	Iofoto | Dreamstime.com
97	Bowie15 | Dreamstime.com
98 Top	© Hedda Gjerpen | iStockphoto.com
98 Bottom	Heysues23 | Dreamstime.com
99	Cynoclub | Dreamstime.com
100	Tuulum | Dreamstime.com
101	Lincolnrogers | Dreamstime.com
102	Fredgoldstein | Dreamstime.com
103	Hkuchera | Dreamstime.com
104 Top	Static85 | Dreamstime.com
104 Bottom	Laures | Dreamstime.com
106	Assignments | Dreamstime.com
107 Bottom	Jeffbanke | Dreamstime.com
107 Top	Blueice69caddy | Dreamstime.com
108	Krzyssagit | Dreamstime.com
109	Kk5hy | Dreamstime.com
110	Asso59 | Dreamstime.com
112 Left	Cleaper | Dreamstime.com
112 Right	Djk | Dreamstime.com
113 Top	A_belov | Dreamstime.com
113 Bottom	Twistntail | Dreamstime.com
114 Left	Corolanty | Dreamstime.com

114 Right	Leigh_341 | Dreamstime.com
115	Igorborodin | Dreamstime.com
116	Swanlake | Dreamstime.com
118	Cynoclub | Dreamstime.com
119	Luis2007 | Dreamstime.com
120	Jayfish | Dreamstime.com
121	Jakezc | Dreamstime.com
122	Paulmaguire | Dreamstime.com
123	Tamarabauer | Dreamstime.com
124	Bobandreev | Dreamstime.com
125	Smileyjoanne | Dreamstime.com
126	Jdazuelos | Dreamstime.com
126	Ankevanwyk | Dreamstime.com
126	Manwolste | Dreamstime.com
126	© Anett Somogyvári | iStockphoto.com
127	Katseyephoto | Dreamstime.com
128	Jimsphotos | Dreamstime.com
128	Weberfoto | Dreamstime.com
128	Lunamarina | Dreamstime.com
128	Galantnie | Dreamstime.com
129	Pirita | Dreamstime.com
131	Edoma | Dreamstime.com
132	Bronwyn8 | Dreamstime.com
133	Index74 | Dreamstime.com
135 Top	Elenathewise | Dreamstime.com
135 Bottom	Shawnjackson | Dreamstime.com
136	© Charles Mann | iStockphoto.com
137	© Michael Westhoff | iStockphoto.com
138	Frantisekp | Dreamstime.com
139	© hughalison | iStockphoto.com
139	© nullplus | iStockphoto.com
140	Murysia | Dreamstime.com
141	Bonniemarie | Dreamstime.com
142	© rusm | iStockphoto.com
143 Top	Projoe | Dreamstime.com
143 Bottom	Gimmi | Dreamstime.com
144	Jack Schiffer | Dreamstime.com
145	Pru1977 | Dreamstime.com
146	Ellende | Dreamstime.com
147	Wildhorsedesigns | Dreamstime.com
148 Top	© Sergio Boccardo iStockphoto.com
148 Bottom	© Charles Mann | iStockphoto.com
149 Top	Tiggra20 | Dreamstime.com
149 Bottom	© MelissaAnneGalleries | iStockphoto.com
150 Top	Bulus | Dreamstime.com
150 Bottom	© Charles Mann | iStockphoto.com
151 Top	Danymages | Dreamstime.com
151 Bottom	Tetordre | Dreamstime.com
152 Top	© Alina Solovyova-Vincent | iStockphoto.com
152 Bottom	© Sylvia Schug | iStockphoto.com
153	Kyslynskyy | Dreamstime.com
154 Top	Bobbigmac | Dreamstime.com
154 Bottom	© Eileen Groome | iStockphoto.com
155	Pwollinga | Dreamstime.com
156	Eriklam | Dreamstime.com
157	Dastin50 | Dreamstime.com
158	Lenora | Dreamstime.com
159	Paulmaguire | Dreamstime.com
160	© Kerstin Klaassen | iStockphoto.com
161	Aginger | Dreamstime.com
162	Jimsphotos | Dreamstime.com
163	Misad | Dreamstime.com
165	Ffennema | Dreamstime.com
166	Iofoto | Dreamstime.com
167	Misad | Dreamstime.com
168	Dizajune | Dreamstime.com
170	Laures | Dreamstime.com
171	Murysia | Dreamstime.com
172	Jacojvr | Dreamstime.com
173	Miolanasvetlana | Dreamstime.com
174	Johnsfon | Dreamstime.com
175	Miraclesmaster | Dreamstime.com
176	Sdankof | Dreamstime.com
178	© John Rich | iStockphoto.com
183	Matteodoria | Dreamstime.com
187	Emicristea | Dreamstime.com
189	Rastan | Dreamstime.com
191	Elenathewise | Dreamstime.com
192	Annieannie | Dreamstime.com

BIBLIOGRAPHY

Vogel, Colin. *Complete Horse Care Manual*. London: Dorling Kindersley Limited, 2003.

Pickeral, Tamsin. *The Horse Lover's Bible.* London: Carol & Brown Publishers, 2008.

Pavia, Audrey, and Janice Posnikoff. *Horses For Dummies.* Indiana: Wiley Publishing, 2005.

Hill, Cherry. *How to Think Like a Horse.* Massachusetts: Storey Publishing, 2006.

Rashid, Mark. *Horses Never Lie.* Devon: David & Charles, 2004.

Gore, Thomas, Paula Gore, James Giffin, and Beth Adelman. *Horse Owner's Veterinary Handbook.* New Jersey: Wiley Publishing, 2008.

Self Bucklin, Gincy. *What Your Horse Wants You to Know.* Indianapolis: Wiley Publishing, 2003.

Rashid, Mark. *Whole Heart, Whole Horse.* New York: Skyhorse Publishing, 2009.

Devereux Smith, Fran. *First Horse.* Colorado: Western Horseman Magazine, 1995.

RESOURCES AND FURTHER INFORMATION:

Greenhawk Harness & Equestrian Supplies (www.greenhawk.ca)

Can-Pro Horse Equipment Ltd. (www.can-prohorseequipment.com)

Cavalier Equestrian (www.cavalier.on.ca)

Tru Hardware, Country Depot, and V and S Department Stores (www.truserv.ca)

Tractor Supply Company (www.tscstores.com)

United Farmers of Alberta (www.ufa.com)

INDEX